King Henry the 4th Part 2

By William Shakespeare

Edited by Julien Coallier

Copyright Julien Coallier 2012

All Rights Reserved.

Characters

Archbishop Scroop, Archbishop of York

Bardolph

Blunt

Brothers

Dancer, speaks the Epilogue

Davy, servant to Shallow

Doll Tearsheet

Earl of Northumberland

Earl of Warwick

Earl of Westmoreland

Edward Poins

Falstaff, Sir John Falstaff

Fang, a Sheriff's officer

First Beadle

First Groom

Francis, a drawer

Francis Feeble, country soldier

Gower

Harcourt

Henry **IV**, King of England

Henry V, Prince, King of England

Hostess Quickly, hostess of a tavern in Eastcheap

Lady Northumberland

Lady Percy

Lord Bardolph

Lord Chief Justice

Lord Hastings

Lord Mowbray

Messenger

Morton, retainer of Northumberland

Page, to Falstaff

Peter Bullcalf, country soldier

Peto

Pistol

Porter

Prince Humphrey, of Goucester

Prince John, of Lancaster

Prince Thomas, Duke of Clarence

Ralph Mouldy, country soldier

Robert Shallow, country Justice

Rumour, the Presenter

Second Beadle

Second Drawer

Second Groom

Servant

Silence, country Justice

Simon Shadow, country soldier

Sir John Colville

Snare, a Sheriff's officer

Third Drawer

Third Groom

Thomas Wart, country soldier

Travers, retainer of Northumberland

Scenes

Intro – Page 9

Act I – Page 11

Scene 1. Warkworth. Before Northumberland's Castle

Scene 2. London. A street

Scene 3. York. The Archbishop's palace

Act II – Page 45

Scene 1. London. A street

Scene 2. London. Another street

Scene 3. Warkworth. Before the castle

Scene 4. London. The Boar's Head Tavern in Eastcheap

Act III – Page 103

Scene 1. Westminster. The palace

Scene 2. Gloucestershire. Before Justice, Shallow's house

Act IV – Page 133

Scene 1. Yorkshire. Within the Forest of Gaultree

Scene 2. Another part of the forest

Scene 3. Another part of the forest

Scene 4. Westminster. The Jerusalem Chamber

Scene 5. Westminster. Another chamber

Act V – Page 183

Scene 1. Gloucestershire. Shallow's house

Scene 2. Westminster. The palace

Scene 3. Gloucestershire. Shallow's orchard

Scene 4. London. A street

Scene 5. Westminster. Near the Abbey

Finally Page - 221

Intro

Warkworth. Before the castle

(Rumour enters, painted full of tongues)

Rumour

Open your ears; for which of you will stop the vent of hearing when loud Rumour speaks?

I, from the orient to the drooping west, making the wind my post-horse, still unfold the acts commenced on this ball of earth, upon my tongues continual slanders ride, the which in every language I pronounce

Stuffing the ears of men with false reports I speak of peace, while covert enmity under the smile of safety wounds the world, and who but Rumour, who but only I, make fearful musters and prepared defence

Whiles the big year, swollen with some other grief is thought with child by the stern tyrant war and no such matter?

Rumour is a pipe blown by surmises, jealousies, conjecture an so easy and so plain a stop that the blunt monster with uncounted heads, the still-discordant wavering multitude, can play upon it.

What need I thus, my well-known body to anatomize among my household? Why is Rumour here?

I run before King Harry's victory

Who in a bloody field by Shrewsbury hath beaten down young Hotspur and his troops, quenching the flame of bold rebellion, even with the rebel's blood

What mean I to speak so true at first?

My office is to noise abroad that Harry Monmouth fell under the wrath of noble Hotspur's sword and that the king before the Douglas' rage stooped his anointed head as low as death.

This have I rumoured through the peasant towns between that royal field of Shrewsbury and this worm-eaten hold of ragged stone, where Hotspur's father, old Northumberland lies crafty-sick

The posts come tiring on and not a man of them brings other news than they have learned of me

From Rumour's tongues they bring smooth comforts false, worse than true wrongs.

(Exits)

Act 1 Scene 1

Warkworth. Before the castle

(Lord Bardolph enters)

Lord Bardolph

Who keeps the gate here, who?

(The Porter opens the gate)

Where is the earl?

Porter

What shall I say you are?

Lord Bardolph

Tell thou the earl that the Lord Bardolph doth attend him here.

Porter

His lordship is walked forth into the orchard

Please it your honour, knock but at the gate and he himself wilt answer.

(Northumberland enters)

Lord Bardolph

Here comes the earl.

(Porter exits)

Northumberland

What news, Lord Bardolph? Every minute now should be the father of some stratagem, the times are wild: contention, like a horse full of high feeding, madly hath broke loose and bears down all before him.

Lord Bardolph

Noble earl, I bring you certain news from Shrewsbury.

Northumberland

Good, and God will!

Lord Bardolph

As good as heart can wish, the king is almost wounded to the death

In the fortune of my lord your son, Prince Harry slain outright

Both the Blunts killed by the hand of Douglas

Young Prince John and Westmoreland and Stafford fled the field

Harry Monmouth's brawn, the hulk Sir John, is prisoner to your son, oh such a day, so fought, so followed and so fairly won, came not till now to dignify the times since Caesar's fortunes!

Northumberland

How is this derived?

Saw you the field? came you from Shrewsbury?

Lord Bardolph

I spake with one, my lord, that came from thence, a gentleman well bred and of good name that freely rendered me these news for true.

Northumberland

Here comes my servant Travers, whom I sent on Tuesday last to listen after news.

(Travers enters)

Lord Bardolph

My lord, I over-rode him on the way

He is furnished with no certainties more than he haply may retail from me.

Northumberland

Now, Travers, what good tidings comes with you?

Travers

My lord, Sir John umfrevile turned me back with joyful tidings

Being better horsed, out-rode me.

After him came spurring hard a gentleman, almost forthspent with speed, that stopped by me to breathe his bloodied horse.

He asked the way to Chester

Of him I did demand what news from Shrewsbury, he told me that rebellion had bad luck and that young Harry Percy's spur was cold.

With that, he gave his able horse the head and bending forward struck his armed heels against the panting sides of his poor jade up to the rowel-head, and starting so he seemed in running to devour the way staying no longer question.

Northumberland

Ha! Again said he young Harry Percy's spur was cold?

Of Hotspur Coldspur? that rebellion had met ill luck?

Lord Bardolph

My lord, I'll tell you what

If my young lord your son have not the day, upon mine honour, for a silken point I'll give my barony, never talk of it.

Northumberland

Why should that gentleman that rode by Travers give then such instances of loss?

Lord Bardolph

Who, he?

He was some hilding fellow that had stolen the horse he rode on, and upon my life, spoke at a venture.

Look, here comes more news.

(Morton enters)

Northumberland

Yea, this man's brow, like to a title-leaf, foretells the nature of a tragic volume, so looks the strand whereon the imperious flood hath left a witnessed usurpation.

Say, Morton, didst thou come from Shrewsbury?

Morton

I ran from Shrewsbury, my noble lord

Where hateful death put on his ugliest mask to fright our party.

Northumberland

How doth my son and brother?

Thou tremblest

The whiteness in thy cheek is apter than thy tongue to tell thy errand.

Even such a man, so faint, so spiritless, so dull, so dead in look, so woe-begone, drew Priam's curtain in the dead of night and would have told him half his Troy was burnt

Priam found the fire ere he his tongue and I my Percy's death were thou report'st it.

This thou wouldst say, your son did thus and thus

Your brother thus, so fought the noble Douglas, stopping my greedy ear with their bold deeds

But in the end, to stop my ear indeed, thou hast a sigh to blow away this praise, ending with brother, son, and all are dead.

Morton

Douglas is living, and your brother, yet

But, for my lord your son…

Northumberland

Why, he is dead.

See what a ready tongue suspicion hath!

He that but fears the thing he would not know hath by instinct knowledge from others' eyes that what he feared is chanced.

Yet speak, Morton

Tell thou an earl his divination liesvqnd I will take it as a sweet disgrace, and make thee rich for doing me such wrong.

Morton

You are too great to be by me gainsaid, your spirit is too true, your fears too certain.

Northumberland

Yet, for all this, say not that Percy's dead.

I see a strange confession in thine eye, thou shakest thy head and hold'st it fear or sin to speak a truth.

If he be slain, say so

The tongue offends not that reports his death and he doth sin that doth believe the dead, not he which says the dead is not alive.

Yet the first bringer of unwelcome news hath but a losing office, and his tongue sounds ever after as a sullen bell, remembered tolling a departing friend.

Lord Bardolph

I cannot think, my lord, your son is dead.

Morton

I am sorry I should force you to believe that which I would to God I had not seen

These mine eyes saw him in bloody state, rendering faint quittance, wearied and out-breathed, to Harry Monmouth

Whose swift wrath beat down the never-daunted Percy to the earth, from whence with life he never more sprung up.

In few, his death, whose spirit lent a fire even to the dullest peasant in his camp, being bruited once, took fire and heat away from the best tempered courage in his troops

For from his metal was his party steeled

Which once in him abated, all the rest turned on themselves, like dull and heavy lead, and as the thing that's heavy in itself upon enforcement flies with greatest speed, so did our men heavy in Hotspur's loss.

Lend to this weight such lightness with their fear that arrows fled not swifter toward their aim, than did our soldiers, aiming at their safety fly from the field.

Then was the noble Worcester too soon taken prisoner

That furious Scot, the bloody Douglas, whose well-labouring sword had three times slain the appearance of the king again vail his stomach and did grace the shame of those that turned their backs, and in his flight, stumbling in fear, was took.

The sum of all is that the king hath won, and hath sent out a speedy power to encounter you, my lord, under the conduct of young Lancaster and Westmoreland.

This is the news at full.

Northumberland

For this I shall have time enough to mourn.

In poison there is physic

These news, having been well, that would have made me sick, being sick, have in some measure made me well

And as the wretch, whose fever-weaken'd joints, like strengthless hinges, buckle under life impatient of his fit, breaks like a fire out of his keeper's arms

Even so my limbs, weaken'd with grief, being now enraged with grief, are thrice themselves.

Hence, therefore, thou nice crutch!

A scaly gauntlet now with joints of steel must glove this hand, and hence, thou sickly quoif!

Thou art a guard too wanton for the head which princes, fleshed with conquest, aim to hit.

Now bind my brows with iron; and approach the ragged'st hour that time and spite dare bring to frown upon the enraged Northumberland!

Let heaven kiss earth! now let not Nature's hand keep the wild flood confined! let order die!

Let this world no longer be a stage to feed contention in a lingering act

Let one spirit of the first-born Cain Reign in all bosoms, that each heart being set on bloody courses, the rude scene may end and darkness be the burier of the dead!

Travers

This strained passion doth you wrong, my lord.

Lord Bardolph

Sweet earl, divorce not wisdom from your honour.

Morton

The lives of all your loving complices

Lean on your health the which, if you give over to stormy passion, must perforce decay.

You cast the event of war, my noble lord, and summed the account of chance, before you said let us make head. It was your presurmise that in the dole of blows, your son might drop

You knew he walked over perils, on an edge, more likely to fall in than to get over

You were advised his flesh was capable of wounds and scars and that his forward spirit would lift him where most trade of danger ranged

Yet did you say go forth

None of this, though strongly apprehended, could restrain the stiff-borne action, what hath then befallen or what hath this bold enterprise brought forth more than that being which was like to be?

Lord Bardolph

We all that are engaged to this loss knew that we ventured on such dangerous seas, that if we wrought our life it was ten to one

Yet we ventured, for the gain proposed choked the respect of likely peril feared

Since we are overset, venture again.

Come, we will all put forth, body and goods.

Morton

It is more than time, and my most noble lord, I hear for certain, and do speak the truth, the gentle Archbishop of York is up with well-appointed powers

He is a man who with a double surety binds his followers.

My lord your son had only but the corpse, but shadows and the shows of men to fight

For that same word, rebellion, did divide the action of their bodies from their souls

They did fight with queasiness, constrained, as men drink potions, that their weapons only seemed on our side

For their spirits and souls, this word: rebellion, it had froze them up as fish are in a pond.

Now the bishop turns insurrection to religion, supposed sincere and holy in his thoughts, he's followed both with body and with mind

Doth enlarge his rising with the blood of fair King Richard, scraped from Pomfret stones

Derives from heaven his quarrel and his cause

Tells them he doth bestride a bleeding land, gasping for life under great Bolingbroke

More and less do flock to follow him.

Northumberland

I knew of this before

To speak truth, this present grief had wiped it from my mind.

Go in with me

Counsel every man the aptest way for safety and revenge

Get posts and letters, and make friends with speed, never so few, and never yet more need.

(Exit)

Act 1 Scene 2

London. A street.

(Falstaff enters with his Page bearing his sword and buckler)

Falstaff

Sirrah, you giant, what says the doctor to my water?

Page

He said, sir, the water itself was a good healthy water;

For the party that owed it, he might have more diseases than he knew for.

Falstaff

Men of all sorts take a pride to gird at me, the brain of this foolish-compounded clay, man, is not able to invent anything that tends to laughter, more than I invent or is invented on me

I am not only witty in myself, but the cause that wit is in other men.

I do here walk before thee like a sow that hath overwhelmed all her litter but one.

If the prince put thee into my service for any other reason than to set me off, why then I have no judgment.

Thou whoreson mandrake, thou art fitter to be worn in my cap than to wait at my heels.

I was never manned with an agate till now, but I will inset you neither in gold nor silver, but in vile apparel, and send you back again to your master for a jewel…

The juvenal, the prince your master, whose chin is not yet fledged.

I will sooner have a beard grow in the palm of my hand than he shall get one on his cheek

Yet he will not stick to say his face is a face-royal, God may finish it when he will, it is not a hair amiss yet

He may keep it still at a face-royal, for a barber shall never earn sixpence out of it

Yet he'll be crowing as if he had writ man ever since his father was a bachelor.

He may keep his own grace, but he's almost out of mine, I can assure him.

What said Master Dombledon about the satin for my short cloak and my slops?

Page

He said, sir, you should procure him better assurance than Bardolph, he would not take his band and yours

He liked not the security.

Falstaff

Let him be damned, like the glutton!

Pray God his tongue be hotter!

A whoreson Achitophel! a rascally yea-forsooth knave!

To bear a gentleman in hand and then stand upon security!

The whoreson smooth-pates do now wear nothing but high shoes, and bunches of keys at their girdles

If a man is through with them in honest taking up, then they must stand upon security.

I had as belief they would put ratsbane in my mouth as offer to stop it with security.

I looked at should have sent me two and twenty yards of satin, as I am a true knight, and he sends me security.

Well, he may sleep in security

He hath the horn of abundance, and the lightness of his wife shines through it, and yet cannot he see, though he have his own lanthorn to light him.

Where's Bardolph?

Page

He's gone into Smithfield to buy your worship a horse.

Falstaff

I bought him in Paul's, and he'll buy me a horse in Smithfield, and I could get me but a wife in the stews, I were manned, horsed, and wived.

(The Lord Chief-Justice and Servant enter)

Page

Sir, here comes the nobleman that committed the Prince for striking him about Bardolph.

Falstaff

Wait, close

I will not see him.

Lord Chief-Justice

What's he that goes there?

Servant

Falstaff, and if it please your lordship.

Lord Chief-Justice

He that was in question for the robbery?

Servant

He, my lord

He hath since done good service at Shrewsbury

As I hear, is now going with some charge to the Lord John of Lancaster.

Lord Chief-Justice

What, to York? Call him back again.

Servant

Sir John Falstaff!

Falstaff

Boy, tell him I am deaf.

Page

You must speak louder; my master is deaf.

Lord Chief-Justice

I am sure he is, to the hearing of anything good.

Go, pluck him by the elbow; I must speak with him.

Servant

Sir John!

Falstaff

What! a young knave, and begging! Is there not wars? Is there not employment? doth not the king lack subjects? Do not the rebels need soldiers? Though it be a shame to be on any side but one, it is worse shame to beg than to be on the worst side, were it worse than the name of rebellion can tell how to make it.

Servant

You mistake me, sir.

Falstaff

Why, sir, did I say you were an honest man? Setting my knighthood and my soldiership aside, I had lied in my throat, if I had said so.

Servant

I pray you, sir, then set your knighthood and our soldiership aside

Give me leave to tell you, you lie in your throat, if you say I am any other than an honest man.

Falstaff

I give thee leave to tell me so! I lay aside that which grows to me! if thou gettest any leave of me, hang me

Thou takest leave, thou wert better be hanged.

You hunt counter: hence! avaunt!

Servant

Sir, my lord would speak with you.

Lord Chief-Justice

Sir John Falstaff, a word with you.

Falstaff

My good lord! God give your lordship good time of day.

I am glad to see your lordship abroad: I heard say your lordship was sick, I hope your lordship goes abroad by advice.

Your lordship, though not clean past your youth, hath yet some smack of age in you, some relish of the saltness of time

I must humbly beseech your lordship to have a reverent care of your health.

Lord Chief-Justice

Sir John, I sent for you before your expedition to Shrewsbury.

Falstaff

An it please your lordship, I hear his majesty is returned with some discomfort from Wales.

Lord Chief-Justice

I talk not of his majesty: you would not come when I sent for you.

Falstaff

And I hear, moreover, his highness is fallen into this same whoreson apoplexy.

Lord Chief-Justice

Well, God mend him! I pray you, let me speak with you.

Falstaff

This apoplexy is, as I take it, a kind of lethargy, and it please your lordship

A kind of sleeping in the blood, a whoreson tingling.

Lord Chief-Justice

What tell you me of it? be it as it is.

Falstaff

It hath its original from much grief, from study and perturbation of the brain, I have read the cause of his effects in Galen, it is a kind of deafness.

Lord Chief-Justice

I think you are fallen into the disease

You hear not what I say to you.

Falstaff

Very well, my lord, very well, rather, and if it please you, it is the disease of not listening, the malady of not marking, that I am troubled withal.

Lord Chief-Justice

To punish you by the heels would amend the attention of your ears; and I care not if I do become your physician.

Falstaff

I am as poor as Job, my lord, but not so patient, your lordship may minister the potion of imprisonment to me in respect of poverty

How should I be your patient to follow your prescriptions, the wise may make some dram of a scruple, or indeed a scruple itself.

Lord Chief-Justice

I sent for you, when there were matters against you for your life, to come speak with me.

Falstaff

As I was then advised by my learned counsel in the laws of this land-service, I did not come.

Lord Chief-Justice

Well, the truth is, Sir John, you live in great infamy.

Falstaff

He that buckles him in my belt cannot live in less.

Lord Chief-Justice

Your means are very slender, and your waste is great.

Falstaff

I would it were otherwise; I would my means were greater, and my waist slenderer.

Lord Chief-Justice

You have misled the youthful prince.

Falstaff

The young prince hath misled me, I am the fellow with the great belly, and he my dog.

Lord Chief-Justice

Well, I am loath to gall a new-healed wound, your day's service at Shrewsbury hath a little gilded over your night's exploit on Gad's-hill, you may thank the unquiet time for your quiet over-posting that action.

Falstaff

My lord?

Lord Chief-Justice

But since all is well, keep it so: wake not a sleeping wolf.

Falstaff

To wake a wolf is as bad as to smell a fox.

Lord Chief-Justice

What! you are as a candle, the better part burnt out.

Falstaff

A wassail candle, my lord, all tallow, if I did say of wax, my growth would approve the truth.

Lord Chief-Justice

There is not a white hair on your face but should have his effect of gravity.

Falstaff

His effect of gravy, gravy, gravy.

Lord Chief-Justice

You follow the young prince up and down, like his ill angel.

Falstaff

Not so, my lord

Your ill angel is light; but I hope he that looks upon me will take me without weighing, and yet in some respects I grant, I cannot go, I cannot tell.

Virtue is of so little regard in these costermonger times that true valour is turned bear-herd, pregnancy is made a tapster, and hath his quick wit wasted in giving reckonings, all the other gifts appertinent to man, as the malice of this age shapes them, are not worth a gooseberry.

You that are old consider not the capacities of us that are young

You do measure the heat of our livers with the bitterness of your galls, and we that are in the vaward of our youth, I must confess, are wags too.

Lord Chief-Justice

Do you set down your name in the scroll of youth, that are written down old with all the characters of age?

Have you not a moist eye? a dry hand? A yellow cheek?

A white beard? a decreasing leg? An increasing belly?

Is not your voice broken? Your wind short?

Your chin double? your wit single?

And every part about you blasted with antiquity?

Will you yet call yourself young? Fie, fie, fie, Sir John!

Falstaff

My lord, I was born about three of the clock in the afternoon, with a white head and something a round belly.

For my voice, I have lost it with halloing and singing of anthems.

To approve my youth further, I will not

The truth is, I am only old in judgment and understanding

He that will caper with me for a thousand marks, let him lend me the money, and have at him!

For the box of the ear that the prince gave you, he gave it like a rude prince and you took it like a sensible lord.

I have chequed him for it, and the young lion repents

Marry, not in ashes and sackcloth, but in new silk and old sack.

Lord Chief-Justice

Well, God send the prince a better companion!

Falstaff

God send the companion a better prince!

I cannot rid my hands of him.

Lord Chief-Justice

Well, the king hath severed you and Prince Harry, I hear you are going with Lord John of Lancaster against the Archbishop and the Earl of Northumberland.

Falstaff

Yea

I thank your pretty sweet wit for it.

But look you pray, all you that kiss my lady peace at home, that our armies join not in a hot day

By the Lord, I take but two shirts out with me, and I mean not to sweat extraordinarily, if it be a hot day and I brandish anything but a bottle, I would, I might never spit white again.

There is not a dangerous action can peep out his head but I am thrust upon it, well, I cannot last ever, but it was always yet the trick of our English nation, if they have a good thing, to make it too common.

If ye will needs say I am an old man, you should give me rest.

I would to God my name were not so terrible to the enemy as it is

I were better to be eaten to death with a rust than to be scoured to nothing with perpetual motion.

Lord Chief-Justice

Well, be honest, be honest; and God bless your expedition!

Falstaff

Will your lordship lend me a thousand pound to furnish me forth?

Lord Chief-Justice

Not a penny, not a penny

You are too impatient to bear crosses.

Fare you well, commend me to my cousin Westmoreland.

(Chief-Justice and Servant exit)

Falstaff

If I do, fillip me with a three-man beetle.

A man can no more separate age and covetousness than all can part young limbs and lechery, but the gout galls the one, and the pox pinches the other

So both the degrees prevent my curses. Boy!

Page

Sir?

Falstaff

What money is in my purse?

Page

Seven groats and two pence.

Falstaff

I can get no remedy against this consumption of the purse, borrowing only lingers and lingers it out, but the disease is incurable.

Go bear this letter to my Lord of Lancaster

To the prince

To the Earl of Westmoreland

This to old Mistress Ursula, whom I have weekly sworn to marry since I perceived the first white hair on my chin

About it, you know where to find me.

(Page exits)

A pox of this gout! or, a gout of this pox! For the one or the other plays the rogue with my great toe.

It is no matter if I do halt

I have the wars for my colour, and my pension shall seem the more reasonable.

A good wit will make use of anything, I will turn diseases to commodity.

(Exits)

Act 1 Scene 3

York. The Archbishop's palace.

(The Archbishop of York, the Lords Hastings, Mowbray, and Bardolph enter)

Archbishop of York

Thus have you heard our cause and known our means

My most noble friends, I pray you all, speak plainly your opinions of our hopes, and first lord marshal, what say you to it?

Mowbray

I well allow the occasion of our arms

Gladly would be better satisfied how in our means we should advance ourselves to look with forehead bold and big enough upon the power and puissance of the king.

Hastings

Our present musters grow upon the file to five and twenty thousand men of choice

Our supplies live largely in the hope of great Northumberland, whose bosom burn with an incensed fire of injuries.

Lord Bardolph

The question then, Lord Hastings, standeth thus

Whether our present five and twenty thousand may hold up head without Northumberland?

Hastings

With him, we may.

Lord Bardolph

Yea, marry, there's the point, but if without him we be thought too feeble, my judgment is, we should not step too far till we had his assistance by the hand

For in a theme so bloody-faced as this conjecture, expectation, and surmise of aids incertain should not be admitted.

Archbishop of York

It is very true, Lord Bardolph

For indeed it was young Hotspur's case at Shrewsbury.

Lord Bardolph

It was, my lord who lined himself with hope eating the air on promise of supply, flattering himself in project of a power much smaller than the smallest of his thoughts, and so, with great imagination proper to madmen, led his powers to death, and winking leaped into destruction.

Hastings

But, by your leave, it never yet did hurt to lay down likelihoods and forms of hope.

Lord Bardolph

Yes, if this present quality of war, indeed the instant action, a cause on foot lives so in hope as in an early spring we see the appearing buds

To prove fruit hope gives not so much warrant as despair that frosts will bite them.

When we mean to build, we first survey the plot, than draw the model

When we see the figure of the house, then must we rate the cost of the erection

If we find outweighs ability, what do we then but draw anew the model in fewer offices, or at last desist to build at all?

Much more, in this great work, which is almost to pluck a kingdom down and set another up, should we survey the plot of situation and the model

Consent upon a sure foundation, question surveyors, know our own estate, how able such a work to undergo to weigh against his opposite

Else we fortify in paper and in figures using the names of men instead of men, like one that draws the model of a house beyond his power to build it

Who, half through, gives over and leaves his part-created cost a naked subject to the weeping clouds and waste for churlish winter's tyranny.

Hastings

Grant that our hopes, yet likely of fair birth, should be still-born, and that we now possessed the utmost man of expectation

I think we are a body strong enough, even as we are, to equal with the king.

Lord Bardolph

What, is the king but five and twenty thousand?

Hastings

To us no more

Nay, not so much, Lord Bardolph.

For his divisions, as the times do brawl, are in three heads, one power against the French, and one against Glendower

Perforce a third must take up us, so is the unfirm king in three divided

His coffers sound with hollow poverty and emptiness.

Archbishop of York

That he should draw his several strengths together and come against us in full puissance, need not be dreaded.

Hastings

If he should do so, he leaves his back unarmed, the French and Welsh

Baying him at the heels, never fear that.

Lord Bardolph

Who is it like should lead his forces hither?

Hastings

The Duke of Lancaster and Westmoreland

Against the Welsh, himself and Harry Monmouth, but who is substituted against the French, I have no certain notice.

Archbishop of York

Let us on and publish the occasion of our arms.

The commonwealth is sick of their own choice

Their over-greedy love hath surfeited, an habitation giddy and unsure hath he that buildeth on the vulgar heart.

Oh thou fond many, with what loud applause didst thou beat heaven with blessing Bolingbroke, before he was what thou wouldst have him be!

And being now trimmed in thine own desires, thou, beastly feeder, art so full of him that thou provokest thyself to cast him up

So, so, thou common dog, didst thou disgorge thy glutton bosom of the royal Richard

Now thou wouldst eat thy dead vomit up, and howl'st to find it.

What trust is in these times?

They that, when Richard lived, would have him die are now become enamoured on his grave, thou, that threw'st dust upon his goodly head when through proud London he came sighing on after the admired heels of Bolingbroke, Crist now oh earth, yield us that king again, and take thou this!

Oh thoughts of men accursed!

Past and to come seems best

Things present worst.

Mowbray

Shall we go draw our numbers and set on?

Hastings

We are time's subjects, and time bids be gone.

(Exit)

Act 2 Scene 1

London. A street.

(Mistress Quickly, Fang and his Boy with her, and Snare following enter)

Mistress Quickly

Master Fang, have you entered the action?

Fang

It is entered.

Mistress Quickly

Where's your woman? Is it a lusty woman? Will all stand to it?

Fang

Sirrah, where's Snare?

Mistress Quickly

Oh Lord, ay! good Master Snare.

Snare

Here, here.

Fang

Snare, we must arrest Sir John Falstaff.

Mistress Quickly

Yea, good Master Snare; I have entered him and all.

Snare

It may chance cost some of us our lives, for he will stab.

Mistress Quickly

Alas the day! take heed of him

He stabbed me in mine own house, and that most beastly, in good faith he cares not what mischief he does.

If his weapon be out, he will bend his will as straw, like any devil

He will spare neither man, woman, nor child.

Fang

If I can close with him, I care not for his thrust.

Mistress Quickly

No, nor I neither: I'll be at your elbow.

Fang

An I but fist him once; and all come but within my vice...

Mistress Quickly

I am undone by his going

I warrant you, he's an infinitive thing upon my score.

Good Master Fang, hold him sure: good Master Snare, let him not escape.

All comes continuantly to Pie-corner—saving your manhoods...

To buy a saddle

He is indited to dinner to the Lubber's-head in Lumbert street, to master Smooth's the silkman

I pray ye, since my exion is entered and my case so openly known to the world, let him be brought in to his answer.

A hundred mark is a long one for a poor lone woman to bear, and I have borne, and borne, and borne, and have been fubbed off, and fubbed off, and fubbed off, from this day to that day, that it is a shame to be thought on.

There is no honesty in such dealing

Unless a woman should be made an ass and a beast, to bear every knave's wrong.

Yonder he comes

That errant malmsey-nose knave, Bardolph, with him

Do your offices, do your offices: Master Fang and Master Snare, do me, do me, do me your offices.

(Falstaff, Page, and Bardolph enter)

Falstaff

How now! whose mare's dead? what's the matter?

Fang

Sir John, I arrest you at the suit of Mistress Quickly.

Falstaff

Away, varlets! Draw, Bardolph: cut me off the villain's head, throw the queen in the channel.

Mistress Quickly

Throw me in the channel! I'll throw thee in the channel.

Wilt thou? wilt thou? thou bastardly rogue!

Murder, murder!

Ah, thou honeysuckle villain!

Wilt thou kill God's officers and the king's?

Ah, thou honey-seed rogue! thou art a honey-seed, a man-queller, and a woman-killer.

Falstaff

Keep them off, Bardolph.

Fang

A rescue! a rescue!

Mistress Quickly

Good people, bring a rescue or two.

Thou wont, wont thou?

Thou wont, wont yee? you, you, thou rogue!

Do, thou hemp-seed!

Falstaff

Away, you scullion! you rampallion!

You fustilarian! I'll tickle your catastrophe.

(The Lord Chief-Justice, and his men enter)

Lord Chief-Justice

What is the matter? keep the peace here, who!

Mistress Quickly

Good my lord, be good to me. I beseech you, stand to me.

Lord Chief-Justice

How now, Sir John! what are you brawling here?

Doth this become your place, your time and business?

You should have been well on your way to York.

Stand from him, fellow, wherefore hang'st upon him?

Mistress Quickly

Oh most worshipful lord, and if it please your grace, I am a poor widow of Eastcheap, and he is arrested at my suit.

Lord Chief-Justice

For what sum?

Mistress Quickly

It is more than for some, my lord

It is for all, all I have.

He hath eaten me out of house and home

He hath put all my substance into that fat belly of his, but I will have some of it out again, or I will ride thee old nights like the mare.

Falstaff

I think I am as like to ride the mare, if I have any vantage of ground to get up.

Lord Chief-Justice

How comes this, Sir John? Fie! what man of good temper would endure this tempest of exclamation?

Are you not ashamed to enforce a poor widow to so rough a course to come by her own?

Falstaff

What is the gross sum that I owe thee?

Mistress Quickly

Marry, if thou wert an honest man, thyself and the money too.

Thou didst swear to me upon a parcel-gilt goblet, sitting in my Dolphin-chamber, at the round table, by a sea-coal fire, upon Wednesday in Wheeson week, when the prince broke thy head for liking his father to a singing-man of Windsor, thou didst swear to me then, as I was washing thy wound, to marry me and make me my lady thy wife. Canst thou deny it?

Did not goodwife Keech, the butcher's wife, come in then and call me gossip Quickly?

Coming in to borrow a mess of vinegar

Telling us she had a good dish of prawns

Whereby thou didst desire to eat some

Whereby I told thee they were ill for a green wound?

And didst thou not, when she was gone down stairs, desire me to be no more so familiarity with such poor people

Saying that ere long they should call me madam?

And didst thou not kiss me and bid me fetch thee thirty shillings?

I put thee now to thy book-oath, deny it, if thou canst.

Falstaff

My lord, this is a poor mad soul; and she says up and down the town that the eldest son is like you, she hath been in good case, and the truth is, poverty hath distracted her.

But for these foolish officers, I beseech you I may have redress against them.

Lord Chief-Justice

Sir John, Sir John, I am well acquainted with your manner of wrenching the true cause the false way.

It is not a confident brow, nor the throng of words that come with such more than impudent sauciness from you, can thrust me from a level consideration, you have, as it appears to me, practised upon the easy-yielding spirit of this woman, and made her serve your uses both in purse and in person.

Mistress Quickly

Yea, in truth, my lord.

Lord Chief-Justice

Pray thee, peace. Pay her the debt you owe her, and unpay the villany you have done her, the one you may do with sterling money, and the other with current repentance.

Falstaff

My lord, I will not undergo this sneap without reply.

You call honourable boldness impudent sauciness, if a man will make courtesy and say nothing, he is virtuous, no, my lord, my humble duty remembered, I will not be your suitor.

I say to you, I do desire deliverance from these officers, being upon hasty employment in the king's affairs.

Lord Chief-Justice

You speak as having power to do wrong, but answer in the effect of your reputation, and satisfy this poor woman.

Falstaff

Come hither, hostess.

(Gower enters)

Lord Chief-Justice

Now, Master Gower, what news?

Gower

The king, my lord, and Harry Prince of Wales are near at hand: the rest the paper tells.

Falstaff

As I am a gentleman.

Mistress Quickly

Faith, you said so before.

Falstaff

As I am a gentleman. Come, no more words of it.

Mistress Quickly

By this heavenly ground I tread on, I must be fain to pawn both my plate and the tapestry of my dining-chambers.

Falstaff

Glasses, glasses is the only drinking: and for thy walls, a pretty slight drollery, or the story of the Prodigal, or the German hunting in water-work, is worth a thousand of these bed-hangings and these fly-bitten tapestries.

Let it be ten pound, if thou canst.

Come, and it were not for thy humours, there's not a better wench in England.

Go, wash thy face, and draw the action.

Come, thou must not be in this humour with me

Dost not know me? come, come, I know thou wast set on to this.

Mistress Quickly

Pray thee, Sir John, let it be but twenty nobles: in faith, I am loath to pawn my plate, so God save me, la!

Falstaff

Let it alone

I'll make other shift: you'll be a fool still.

Mistress Quickly

Well, you shall have it, though I pawn my gown.

I hope you'll come to supper.

You'll pay me all together?

Falstaff

Will I live?

(To Bardolph)

Go, with her, with her

Hook on, hook on.

Mistress Quickly

Will you have Doll Tearsheet meet you at supper?

Falstaff

No more words; let's have her.

(Mistress Quickly, Bardolph, Officers and Boy enter)

Lord Chief-Justice

I have heard better news.

Falstaff

What's the news, my lord?

Lord Chief-Justice

Where lay the king last night?

Gower

At Basingstoke, my lord.

Falstaff

I hope, my lord, all's well, what is the news, my lord?

Lord Chief-Justice

Come all his forces back?

Gower

No, fifteen hundred foot, five hundred horse are marched up to my lord of Lancaster, against Northumberland and the Archbishop.

Falstaff

Comes the king back from Wales, my noble lord?

Lord Chief-Justice

You shall have letters of me presently, come, go along with me, good Master Gower.

Falstaff

My lord!

Lord Chief-Justice

What's the matter?

Falstaff

Master Gower, shall I entreat you with me to dinner?

Gower

I must wait upon my good lord here

I thank you, good Sir John.

Lord Chief-Justice

Sir John, you loiter here too long, being you are to take soldiers up in counties as you go.

Falstaff

Will you sup with me, Master Gower?

Lord Chief-Justice

What foolish master taught you these manners, Sir John?

Falstaff

Master Gower, if they become me not, he was a fool that taught them me.

This is the right fencing grace, my lord

Tap for tap, and so part fair.

Lord Chief-Justice

Now the Lord lighten thee! thou art a great fool.

(Exit)

Act 2 Scene 2

London. Another street.

(Prince Henry and Poins enter)

Prince Henry

Before God, I am exceeding weary.

Poins

Is it come to that?

I had thought weariness durst not have attached one of so high blood.

Prince Henry

Faith, it does me; though it discolours the complexion of my greatness to acknowledge it.

Doth it not show vilely in me to desire small beer?

Poins

Why, a prince should not be so loosely studied as to remember so weak a composition.

Prince Henry

Belike then my appetite was not princely got

By my troth, I do now remember the poor creature, small beer.

But, indeed these humble considerations make me out of love with my greatness.

What a disgrace is it to me to remember thy name! or to know thy face to-morrow! or to take note how many pair of silk stockings thou hast, viz. these, and those that were thy peach-coloured ones! or to bear the inventory of thy shirts, as, one for superfluity, and another for use!

But that the tennis-court-keeper knows better than I

For it is a low ebb of linen with thee when thou keepest not racket there; as thou hast not done a great while, because the rest of thy low countries have made a shift to eat up thy Holland, and God knows, whether those that bawl out the ruins of thy linen shall inherit his kingdom, but the midwives say the children are not in the fault

Whereupon the world increases, and kindreds are mightily strengthened

Poins

How will it follows, after you have laboured so hard, you should talk so idly!

Tell me, how many good young princes would do so, their fathers being so sick as yours at this time is?

Prince Henry

Shall I tell thee one thing, Poins?

Poins

Yes, faith, and let it be an excellent good thing.

Prince Henry

It shall serve among wits of no higher breeding than thine.

Poins

Go to

I stand the push of your one thing that you will tell.

Prince Henry

Marry, I tell thee, it is not meet that I should be sad, now my father is sick

Albeit I could tell thee, as to one it pleases me, for fault of a better to call my friend, I could be sad, and sad indeed too.

Poins

Very hardly upon such a subject.

Prince Henry

By this hand thou thinkest me as far in the devil's book as thou and Falstaff for obduracy and persistency, let the end try the man.

But I tell thee, my heart bleeds inwardly that my father is so sick, and keeping such vile company as thou art hath in reason taken from me all ostentation of sorrow.

Poins

The reason?

Prince Henry

What wouldst thou think of me, if I should weep?

Poins

I would think thee a most princely hypocrite.

Prince Henry

It would be every man's thought; and thou art a blessed fellow to think as every man thinks, never a man's thought in the world keeps the road-way better than thine, every man would think me an hypocrite indeed.

And what cites your most worshipful thought to think so?

Poins

Why, because you have been so lewd and so much engraffed to Falstaff.

Prince Henry

And to thee.

Poins

By this light, I am well spoke on

I can hear it with my own ears, the worst that they can say of me is that I am a second brother and that I am a proper fellow of my hands

Those two things, I confess, I cannot help.

By the mass, here comes Bardolph.

(Bardolph and Page enter)

Prince Henry

And the boy that I gave Falstaff, all had him from me Christian, and look if the fat villain have not transformed him ape.

Bardolph

God save your grace!

Prince Henry

And yours, most noble Bardolph!

Bardolph

Come, you virtuous ass, you bashful fool, must you be blushing? wherefore blush you now?

What a maidenly man-at-arms are you become!

Is it such a matter to get a pottle-pot's maidenhead?

Page

A' calls me even now, my lord, through a red lattice, and I could discern no part of his face from the window, at last I spied his eyes and methought he had made two holes in the ale-wife's new petticoat and so peeped through.

Prince Henry

Has not the boy profited?

Bardolph

Away, you whoreson upright rabbit, away!

Page

Away, you rascally Althaea's dream, away!

Prince Henry

Instruct us, boy

What dream, boy?

Page

Marry, my lord, Althaea dreamed she was delivered of a fire-brand

Therefore I call him her dream.

Prince Henry

A crown's worth of good interpretation, there it is, boy.

Poins

Oh, that this good blossom could be kept from cankers!

Well, there is sixpence to preserve thee.

Bardolph

An you do not make him hanged among you, the gallows shall have wrong.

Prince Henry

And how doth thy master, Bardolph?

Bardolph

Well, my lord. He heard of your grace's coming to town, there's a letter for you.

Poins

Delivered with good respect.

And how doth the martlemas, your master?

Bardolph

In bodily health, sir.

Poins

Marry, the immortal part needs a physician

That moves not him, though that be sick it dies not.

Prince Henry

I do allow this wen to be as familiar with me as my dog

He holds his place, for look you how be writes.

Poins

(Reads) John Falstaff, knight…

Every man must know that, as often as he has occasion to name himself, even like those that are kin to the king

They never prick their finger but they say, there's some of the king's blood spilt.

How comes that? says he, that takes upon him not to conceive.

The answer is as ready as a borrower's cap, I am the king's poor cousin, sir.

Prince Henry

Nay, they will be kin to us, or they will fetch it from Jupiter's alphabet, but to the letter.

Poins

(Reads) Sir John Falstaff, knight, to the son of the king, nearest his father, Harry Prince of Wales, greeting.

Why, this is a certificate.

Prince Henry

Peace!

Poins

(Reads) I will imitate the honourable Romans in brevity, he sure means brevity in breath, short-winded.

I commend me to thee, I commend thee and I leave thee.

Be not too familiar with Poins

He misuses thy favours so much, that he swears thou art to marry his sister Nell.

Repent at idle times as thou mayest

So, farewell.

Thine, by yea and no, which is as much as to say, as thou use him, John Falstaff with my familiars, John with my brothers and sisters, and Sir John with all Europe.

My lord, I'll steep this letter in sack and make him eat it.

Prince Henry

That's to make him eat twenty of his words.

But do you use me thus, Ned? must I marry your sister?

Poins

God send the wench no worse fortune! But I never said so.

Prince Henry

Well, thus we play the fools with the time, and the spirits of the wise sit in the clouds and mock us.

Is your master here in London?

Bardolph

Yea, my lord.

Prince Henry

Where suppers he? doth the old boar feed in the old frank?

Bardolph

At the old place, my lord, in Eastcheap.

Prince Henry

What company?

Page

Ephesians, my lord, of the old church.

Prince Henry

Supper any women with him?

Page

None, my lord, but old Mistress Quickly and Mistress Doll Tearsheet.

Prince Henry

What pagan may that be?

Page

A proper gentlewoman, sir, and a kinswoman of my master's

Prince Henry

Even such kin as the parish heifers are to the town

bull.

Shall we steal upon them, Ned, at supper?

Poins

I am your shadow, my lord

I'll follow you.

Prince Henry

Sirrah, you boy, and Bardolph, no word to your master that I am yet come to town, there's for your silence.

Bardolph

I have no tongue, sir.

Page

And for mine, sir, I will govern it.

Prince Henry

Fare you well

Go.

(Bardolph and Page exit)

This Doll Tearsheet should be some road.

Poins

I warrant you, as common as the way between Saint Alban's and London.

Prince Henry

How might we see Falstaff bestow himself to-night in his true colours, and not ourselves be seen?

Poins

Put on two leathern jerkins and aprons, and wait upon him at his table as drawers.

Prince Henry

From a God to a bull? a heavy decension! It was

Jupiter's case.

From a prince to an apprentice?

A low transformation!

That shall be mine

In everything the purpose must weigh with the folly.

Follow me, Ned.

(Exit)

Act 2 Scene 3

Warkworth. Before the castle.

(Northumberland, Lady Northumberland, and Lady Percy enter)

Northumberland

I pray thee, loving wife, and gentle daughter, give even way unto my rough affairs, put not you on the visage of the times and be like them to Percy troublesome.

Lady

Northumberland

I have given over, I will speak no more, do what you will

Your wisdom be your guide.

Northumberland

Alas, sweet wife, my honour is at pawn

But my going, nothing can redeem it.

Lady Percy

Oh yet, for God's sake, go not to these wars!

The time was, father, that you broke your word, when you were more endeared to it than now

When your own Percy, when my heart's dear Harry, threw many a northward look to see his father bring up his powers

He did long in vain.

Who then persuaded you to stay at home?

There were two honours lost, yours and your son's.

For yours, the God of heaven brighten it!

For his, it stuck upon him as the sun in the grey vault of heaven, and by his light did all the chivalry of England move to do brave acts, he was indeed the glass wherein the noble youth did dress themselves

He had no legs that practised not his gait, and speaking thick, which nature made his blemish, became the accents of the valiant

For those that could speak low and tardily would turn their own perfection to abuse, to seem like him so that in speech, in gait, in diet, in affections of delight, in military rules, humours of blood, he was the mark and glass, copy and book that fashioned others.

And him, oh wondrous him!

Oh miracle of men! him did you leave, second to none, unseconded by you, to look upon the hideous god of war in disadvantage

To abide a field where nothing but the sound of Hotspur's name did seem defensible: so you left him

Never, oh never, do his ghost the wrong to hold your honour more precise and nice with others than with him!

Let them alone, the marshal and the archbishop are strong, had my sweet Harry had but half their numbers, to-day might I, hanging on Hotspur's neck, have talked of Monmouth's grave.

Northumberland

Beshrew your heart, fair daughter, you do draw my spirits from me with new lamenting ancient oversights.

But I must go and meet with danger there, or it will seek me in another place and find me worse provided.

Lady Northumberland

Oh, fly to Scotland, till that the nobles and the armed commons have of their puissance made a little taste.

Lady Percy

If they get ground and vantage of the king, then join you with them like a rib of steel to make strength stronger

For all our loves, first let them try themselves.

So did your son

He was so suffered, so came I a widow

Never shall have length of life enough to rain upon remembrance with mine eyes, that it may grow and sprout as high as heaven for recordation to my noble husband.

Northumberland

Come, come, go in with me.

It is with my mind, as with the tide swelled up unto his height, that makes a still-stand, running neither way, fain would I go to meet the archbishop, but many thousand reasons hold me back.

I will resolve for Scotland, there am I, till time and vantage crave my company.

(Exit)

Act 2 Scene 4

London. The Boar's-head Tavern in Eastcheap.

(Two Drawers enter)

First Drawer

What the devil hast thou brought there? apple-johns?

thou knowest Sir John cannot endure an apple-john.

Second Drawer

Mass, thou sayest true.

The prince once set a dish of apple-johns before him, and told him there were five more Sir Johns, and, putting off his hat, said I will now take my leave of these six dry, round, old, withered knights.

It angered him to the heart, but he hath forgot that.

First Drawer

Why, then, cover, and set them down, and see if thou canst find out Sneak's noise

Mistress Tearsheet would fain hear some music.

Dispatch, the room where they supper'd is too hot

They'll come in straight.

Second Drawer

Sirrah, here will be the prince and Master Poins anon

They will put on two of our jerkins and aprons

Sir John must not know of it, Bardolph hath brought word.

First Drawer

By the mass, here will be old Utis, it will be an excellent stratagem.

Second Drawer

I'll see if I can find out Sneak.

(Exits)

(Mistress Quickly and Doll Tearsheet enter)

Mistress Quickly

In good faith, sweetheart, methinks now you are in an excellent good temporality, your pulsidge beats as extraordinarily as heart would desire

Your colour, I warrant you, is as red as any rose, in good truth, la!

But, in good faith faith, you have drunk too much canaries

That's a marvellous searching wine, and it perfumes the blood ere one can say what's this? How do you now?

Doll Tearsheet

Better than I was, them!

Mistress Quickly

Why, that's well said

A good heart's worth gold.

Lord, here comes Sir John.

(Falstaff enters)

Falstaff

(Singing) When Arthur first in court

…Empty the jordan.

(First Drawer exits)

(Singing)

…And was a worthy king.

How now, Mistress Doll!

Mistress Quickly

Sick of a calm

Yea, good faith

Falstaff

So is all her sect

They be once in a calm, they are sick.

Doll Tearsheet

You muddy rascal, is that all the comfort you give me?

Falstaff

You make fat rascals, Mistress Doll.

Doll Tearsheet

I make them! gluttony and diseases make them

I make them not.

Falstaff

If the cook help to make the gluttony, you help to make the diseases, Doll, we catch of you, Doll, we catch of you

Grant that, my poor virtue grant that.

Doll Tearsheet

Yea, joy, our chains and our jewels.

Falstaff

Your broaches, pearls, and ouches, for to serve bravely is to come halting off, you know, to come off the breach with his pike bent bravely, and to surgery bravely

To venture upon the charged chambers bravely...

Doll Tearsheet

Hang yourself, you muddy conger, hang yourself!

Mistress Quickly

By my troth, this is the old fashion

You two never meet but you fall to some discord, you are both, in good truth, as rheumatic as two dry toasts

You cannot one bear with another's confirmities.

What the good-year! One must bear, and that must be you, you are the weaker vessel, as they say, the emptier vessel.

Doll Tearsheet

Can a weak empty vessel bear such a huge full hogshead?

There's a whole merchant's venture of Bourdeaux stuff in him

You have not seen a hulk better stuffed in the hold.

Come, I'll be friends with thee, Jack, thou art going to the wars

Whether I shall ever see thee again or no, there is nobody cares.

(First Drawer re-enters)

First Drawer

Sir, Ancient Pistol's below, and would speak with you.

Doll Tearsheet

Hang him, swaggering rascal!

Let him not come hither, it is the foul-mouthed'st rogue in England.

Mistress Quickly

If he swagger, let him not come here, no, by my faith

I must live among my neighbours: I'll no swaggerers, I am in good name and fame with the very best, shut the door

There comes no swaggerers here, I have not lived all this while, to have swaggering now, shut the door, I pray you.

Falstaff

Dost thou hear, hostess?

Mistress Quickly

Pray yee, pacify yourself, Sir John, there comes no swaggerers here.

Falstaff

Dost thou hear? it is mine ancient.

Mistress Quickly

Tilly-fally, Sir John, never tell me

Your ancient swaggerer comes not in my doors.

I was before Master till sick, the debuty, the other day

As he said to me, it was no longer ago than Wednesday last, I in good faith, neighbour Quickly, says he

Master Dumbe, our minister, was by then

Neighbour Quickly, says he, receive those that are civil

For, said he, you are in an ill name, now all said so, I can tell whereupon

Says he, you are an honest woman, and well thought on

Take heed what guests you receive, receive, says he, no swaggering companions.

There comes none here, you would bless you to hear what he said, no, I'll no swaggerers.

Falstaff

He's no swaggerer, hostess

A tame cheater, with faith

You may stroke him as gently as a puppy greyhound, he'll not swagger with a Barbary hen, if her feathers turn back in any show of resistance.

Call him up, drawer.

(First Drawer exits)

Mistress Quickly

Cheater, call you him? I will bar no honest man my house, nor no cheater

I do not love swaggering, by my troth

I am the worse, when one says swagger, feel, masters, how I shake

Look you, I warrant you.

Doll Tearsheet

So you do, hostess.

Mistress Quickly

Do I? yea, in very truth, do I, and it were an aspen leaf I cannot abide swaggerers.

(Pistol, Bardolph, and Page enter)

Pistol

God save you, Sir John!

Falstaff

Welcome, Ancient Pistol.

Here, Pistol, I charge you with a cup of sack, do you discharge upon mine hostess.

Pistol

I will discharge upon her, Sir John, with two bullets.

Falstaff

She is Pistol-proof, sir, you shall hardly offend her.

Mistress Quickly

Come, I'll drink no proofs nor no bullets, I'll drink no more than will do me good, for no man's pleasure, I.

Pistol

Then to you, Mistress Dorothy

I will charge you.

Doll Tearsheet

Charge me! I scorn you, scurvy companion.

What! you poor, base, rascally, cheating, lack-linen mate!

Away, you mouldy rogue, away!

I am meat for your master.

Pistol

I know you, Mistress Dorothy.

Doll Tearsheet

Away, you cut-purse rascal!

You filthy bung, away!

By this wine, I'll thrust my knife in your mouldy chaps, and you play the saucy cuttle with me.

Away, you bottle-ale rascal!

You basket-hilt stale juggler, you!

Since when, I pray you, sir? God's light, with two points on your shoulder? much!

Pistol

God let me not live, but I will murder your ruff for this.

Falstaff

No more, Pistol

I would not have you go off here, discharge yourself of our company, Pistol.

Mistress Quickly

No, Good Captain Pistol

Not here, sweet captain.

Doll Tearsheet

Captain! thou abominable damned cheater, art thou not ashamed to be called captain?

And captains were of my mind, they would truncheon you out, for taking their names upon you before you have earned them.

You a captain! you slave, for what?

For tearing a poor whore's ruff in a bawdy-house?

He a captain! hang him, rogue! he lives upon mouldy stewed prunes and dried cakes.

A captain! God's light, these villains will make the word as odious as the word occupy

Which was an excellent good word before it was ill sorted, therefore captains had need look to it.

Bardolph

Pray thee, go down, good ancient.

Falstaff

Hark thee hither, Mistress Doll.

Pistol

Not I, I tell thee what, Corporal Bardolph, I could tear her, I'll be revenged of her.

Page

Pray thee, go down.

Pistol

I'll see her damned first; to Pluto's damned lake, by this hand, to the infernal deep, with Erebus and tortures vile also.

Hold hook and line, say I.

Down, down, dogs! down, faitors!

Have we not Hiren here?

Mistress Quickly

Good Captain Peesel, be quiet; it is very late, in faith, I beseek you now, aggravate your choler.

Pistol

These be good humours, indeed!

Shall pack-horses and hollow pampered jades of Asia, which cannot go but thirty mile a-day, compare with Caesars, and with Cannibals, and Trojan Greeks?

Nay, rather damn them with King Cerberus

Let the welkin roar.

Shall we fall foul for toys?

Mistress Quickly

By my troth, captain, these are very bitter words.

Bardolph

Be gone, good ancient, this will grow to abrawl anon.

Pistol

Die men like dogs! give crowns like pins!

Have we not Helen here?

Mistress Quickly

Oh my word, captain, there's none such here.

What the good-year! Do you think I would deny her?

For God's sake, be quiet.

Pistol

Then feed, and be fat, my fair Calipolis.

Come, give's some sack.

If fortune torments, hope does contents me.

Fear we broadsides?

No, let the fiend give fire, give me some sack and sweetheart, lie thou there.

(Laying down his sword)

Come we to full points here and are the others absent as nothing?

Falstaff

Pistol, I would be quiet.

Pistol

Sweet knight, I kiss thy neaf

What we have seen are the seven stars.

Doll Tearsheet

For God's sake, thrust him down stairs, I cannot endure such a fustian rascal.

Pistol

Thrust him down stairs! know we not Galloway nags?

Falstaff

Quite him down Bardolph, like a shove-groat shilling, nay, and all do nothing but speak nothing, all shall be nothing here.

Bardolph

Come, get you down stairs.

Pistol

What! shall we have incision? shall we imbrue?

(Snatching up his sword)

Then death rock me asleep, abridge my doleful days!

Why then, let grievous, ghastly, gaping wounds untwine the Sisters Three!

Come, Atropos, I say!

Mistress Quickly

Here's goodly stuff toward!

Falstaff

Give me my rapier, boy.

Doll Tearsheet

I pray thee, Jack, I pray thee, do not draw.

Falstaff

Get you down stairs.

(Drawing, and driving Pistol out)

Mistress Quickly

Here's a goodly tumult!

I'll forswear keeping house, before I'll be in these territs and frights so.

Murder, I warrant now.

Alas, alas! put up your naked weapons, put up your naked weapons.

(Pistol and Bardolph exit)

Doll Tearsheet

I pray thee, Jack, be quiet; the rascal's gone.

Ah, you whoreson little valiant villain, you!

Mistress Quickly

He, you are not hurt in the groin? methought a' made a shrewd thrust at your belly.

(Bardolph re-enters)

Falstaff

Have you turned him out of doors?

Bardolph

Yea, sir.

The rascal's drunk, you have hurt him sir, in the shoulder.

Falstaff

A rascal! to brave me!

Doll Tearsheet

Ah, you sweet little rogue, you!

Alas poor ape, how thou sweatest!

Come, let me wipe thy face

ome on, you whoreson chops, ah, rogue!

In faith, I love thee, thou art as valorous as Hector of Troy, worth five of Agamemnon, and ten times better than the Nine Worthies, ah villain!

Falstaff

A rascally slave! I will toss the rogue in a blanket.

Doll Tearsheet

Does thou darest for thy heart, and thou dost, I'll canvass thee between a pair of sheets.

(Music enters)

Page

The music is come, sir.

Falstaff

Let them play.

Play, sirs.

Sit on my knee, Doll.

A rascal bragging slave!

The rogue fled from me like quicksilver.

Doll Tearsheet

In good faith, and thou followedst him like a church.

Thou whoreson little tidy Bartholomew boar-pig, when wilt thou leave fighting old days and meddling old nights, and begin to patch up thine old body for heaven?

(Prince Henry and Poins enter behind, disguised)

Falstaff

Peace, good Doll! do not speak like a death's-head

Do not bid me remember mine end.

Doll Tearsheet

Sirrah, what humour's the prince of?

Falstaff

A good shallow young fellow, a' would have made a good pantler, a' would have chipped bread well.

Doll Tearsheet

They say Poins has a good wit.

Falstaff

He a good wit? Hang him, baboon!

His wit's as thick as Tewksbury mustard

There's no more conceit in him than is in a mallet.

Doll Tearsheet

Why does the prince love him so, then?

Falstaff

Because their legs are both of a bigness, and a' plays at quoits well, and eats conger and fennel, and drinks off candles' ends for flap-dragons, and rides the wild-mare with the boys, and jumps upon joined-stools, and swears with a good grace, and wears his boots very smooth, like unto the sign of the leg, and breeds no bate with telling of discreet stories

Such other gambol faculties have, that show a weak mind and an able body, for the which the prince admits him, for the prince himself is such another

The weight of a hair will turn the scales between their avoirdupois.

Prince Henry

Would not this nave of a wheel have his ears cut off?

Poins

Let's beat him before his whore.

Prince Henry

Look, whether the withered elder hath not his poll clawed like a parrot.

Poins

Is it not strange that desire should so many years outlive performance?

Falstaff

Kiss me, Doll.

Prince Henry

Saturn and Venus this year in conjunction!

What says the almanac to that?

Poins

And look, whether the fiery Trigon, his man, be not lisping to his master's old tables, his note-book, his counsel-keeper.

Falstaff

Thou dost give me flattering busses.

Doll Tearsheet

By my troth, I kiss thee with a most constant heart.

Falstaff

I am old, I am old.

Doll Tearsheet

I love thee better than I love e'er a scurvy young boy of them all.

Falstaff

What stuff wilt have a kirtle of? I shall receive money of Thursday, shalt have a cap to-morrow.

A merry song come, it grows late

We'll to bed.

Thou'lt forget me when I am gone.

Doll Tearsheet

By my troth, thou'lt set me a-weeping, and thou sayest so, prove that ever I dress myself handsome till thy return, well, harken at the end.

Falstaff

Some sack, Francis.

Prince Henry Poins

Anon, anon, sir.

(Coming forward)

Falstaff

Ha! a bastard son of the king's? And art not thou Poins his brother?

Prince Henry

Why, thou globe of sinful continents!

What a life dost thou lead!

Falstaff

A better than thou: I am a gentleman; thou art a drawer.

Prince Henry

Very true, sir

I come to draw you out by the ears.

Mistress Quickly

Oh, the Lord preserve thy good grace! by my troth, welcome to London.

Now, the Lord bless that sweet face of thine!

Oh Jesus, are you come from Wales?

Falstaff

Thou whoreson mad compound of majesty, by this light flesh and corrupt blood, thou art welcome.

Doll Tearsheet

How, you fat fool! I scorn you.

Poins

My lord, he will drive you out of your revenge and turn all to a merriment, if you take not the heat.

Prince Henry

You whoreson candle-mine, you, how vilely did you speak of me even now before this honest, virtuous, civil gentlewoman!

Mistress Quickly

God's blessing of your good heart! and so she is, by my troth.

Falstaff

Didst thou hear me?

Prince Henry

Yea, and you knew me, as you did when you ran away

by God's-hill, you knew I was at your back and spoke it on purpose to try my patience.

Falstaff

No, no, no; not so.

I did not think thou wast within hearing.

Prince Henry

I shall drive you then to confess the wilful abuse

Then I know how to handle you.

Falstaff

No abuse, Hal, of mine honour, no abuse.

Prince Henry

Not to dispraise me, and call me pantier and bread-chipper and I know not what?

Falstaff

No abuse, Hal.

Poins

No abuse?

Falstaff

No abuse, Ned in the world

Honest Ned, none.

I dispraised him before the wicked, that the wicked might not fall in love with him

I have done the part of a careful friend and a true subject, and thy father is to give me thanks for it.

No abuse Hal, none, Ned, none, no faith boys, none.

Prince Henry

See now, whether pure fear and entire cowardice doth not make thee wrong this virtuous gentlewoman to close with us? is she of the wicked?

Is thine hostess here of the wicked?

Or is thy boy of the wicked?

Or honest Bardolph, whose zeal burns in his nose, of the wicked?

Poins

Answer, thou dead elm, answer.

Falstaff

The fiend hath pricked down Bardolph irrecoverable

His face is Lucifer's privy-kitchen, where he doth nothing but roast malt-worms.

For the boy, there is a good angel about him

The devil outbids him too.

Prince Henry

For the women?

Falstaff

For one of them, she is in hell already, and burns poor souls.

For the other, I owe her money, and whether she be damned for that, I know not.

Mistress Quickly

No, I warrant you.

Falstaff

No, I think thou art not

I think thou art quit for that.

Marry, there is another indictment upon thee for suffering flesh to be eaten in thy house, contrary to the law

For the which I think thou wilt howl.

Mistress Quickly

All victuallers do so

What's a joint of mutton or two in a whole Lent?

Prince Henry

You, gentlewoman…

Doll Tearsheet

What says your grace?

Falstaff

His grace says that which his flesh rebels against.

(Knocking within)

Mistress Quickly

Who knocks so loud at door? Look to the door there, Francis.

(Peto enters)

Prince Henry

Peto, how now! what news?

Peto

The king your father is at Westminster and there are twenty weak and wearied posts come from the north: and, as I came along, I met and overtook a dozen captains, bare-headed, sweating, knocking at the taverns and asking everyone for Sir John Falstaff.

Prince Henry

By heaven, Poins, I feel me much to blame, so idly to profane the precious time, when tempest of commotion, like the south borne with black vapour, doth begin to melt and drop upon our bare unarmed heads.

Give me my sword and cloak.

Falstaff, good night.

(Poins, Peto and Bardolph exit)

Falstaff

Now comes in the sweetest morsel of the night and we must hence and leave it unpicked.

(Knocking within)

More knocking at the door!

(Bardolph re-enters)

How now! what's the matter?

Bardolph

You must away to court, sir, presently

A dozen captains stay at door for you.

Falstaff

(To the Page) Pay the musicians, sirrah. Farewell, hostess.

Farewell, Doll.

You see, my good wenches, how men of merit are sought after: the undeserver may sleep, when the man of action is called on.

Farewell good wenches, if I be not sent away post, I will see you again ere I go.

Doll Tearsheet

I cannot speak; if my heart be not read to burst...

Well, sweet Jack, have a care of thyself.

Falstaff

Farewell, farewell.

(Falstaff and **Bardolph exits)**

Mistress Quickly

Well, fare thee well, I have known thee these twenty-nine years, come peascod-time

An honester and truer-hearted man...

Well, fare thee well.

Bardolph

(Within) Mistress Tearsheet!

Mistress Quickly

What's the matter?

Bardolph

(Within) Good Mistress Tearsheet, come to my master.

Mistress Quickly

Oh run Doll, run

Run good Doll, come.

(She comes blubbered)

Yea, will you come, Doll?

(Exit)

Act 3 Scene 1

Westminster. The palace.

(King Henry IV enters in his nightgown, with a Page)

King Henry IV

Go call the Earls of Surrey and of Warwick

Here they come, bid them over-read these letters, and well consider of them; make good speed.

(Page exits)

How many thousand of my poorest subjects are at this hour asleep!

Oh sleep, Oh gentle sleep, nature's soft nurse, how have I frighted thee, that thou no more wilt weigh my eyelids down and steep my senses in forgetfulness?

Why rather, sleep, liest thou in smoky cribs, upon uneasy pallets stretching thee and hushed with buzzing night-flies to thy slumber,

Than in the perfumed chambers of the great, under the canopies of costly state, and lulled with sound of sweetest melody?

Oh thou dull god, why liest thou with the vile in loathsome beds, and leavest the kingly couch a watch-case or a common 'larum-bell?

Wilt thou upon the high and giddy mast seal up the ship-boy's eyes, and rock his brains in cradle of the rude imperious surge, and in the visitation of the winds who take the ruffian billows by the top,

Curling their monstrous heads and hanging them with deafening clamour in the slippery clouds, that with the hurly, death itself awakes?

Canst thou, oh partial sleep, give thy repose to the wet sea-boy in an hour so rude and in the calmest and most stillest night

With all appliances and means to boot, deny it to a king?

Then happy low, lie down!

Uneasy lies the head that wears a crown.

(Warkwick and Surrey enter)

Warkwick

Many good morrows to your majesty!

King Henry IV

Is it good morrow, lords?

Warkwick

It is one o'clock, and past.

King Henry IV

Why, then, good morrow to you all, my lords.

Have you read over the letters that I sent you?

Warkwick

We have, my liege.

King Henry IV

Then you perceive the body of our kingdom, how foul it is

What rank diseases grow and with what danger, near the heart of it.

Warkwick

It is but as a body yet distempered

Which to his former strength may be restored with good advice and little medicine, my Lord Northumberland will soon be cooled.

King Henry IV

Oh God! that one might read the book of fate and see the revolution of the times make mountains level and the continent, weary of solid firmness, melt itself into the sea!

And other times, to see the beachy girdle of the ocean too wide for Neptune's hips

How chances mock, and changes fill the cup of alteration with divers liquors!

Oh, if this were seen, the happiest youth, viewing his progress through what perils past, what crosses to ensue, would shut the book and sit him down and die.

It is not yet ten years gone since Richard and Northumberland, great friends, did feast together, and in two years after were they at wars it is but eight years since this Percy was the man nearest my soul.

Who like a brother toiled in my affairs and laid his love and life under my foot, yea, for my sake, even to the eyes of Richard gave him defiance.

But which of you was by…

You, cousin Nevil, as I may remember…

(To Warkwick)

When Richard, with his eye brimful of tears, then chequeed and rated by Northumberland, did speak these words, now proved a prophecy?

Northumberland, thou ladder by the which my cousin Bolingbroke ascends my throne

Though then, God knows, I had no such intent, but that necessity so bowed the state that I and greatness were compelled to kiss, in the time shall come and thus did he follow it

The time will come that foul sin, gathering head, shall break into corruption, so went on, foretelling this same time's condition and the division of our amity.

Warkwick

There is a history in all men's lives, figuring the nature of the times deceased

The which observed, a man may prophesy, with a near aim, of the main chance of things as yet not come to life, which in their seeds and weak beginnings lie intreasured.

Such things become the hatch and brood of time

By the necessary form of this King Richard might create a perfect guess that great Northumberland, then false to him, would of that seed grow to a greater falseness

Which should not find a ground to root upon, unless on you.

King Henry IV

Are these things then necessities?

Then let us meet them like necessities, and that same word even now cries out on us, they say the bishop and Northumberland are fifty thousand strong.

Warkwick

It cannot be, my lord

Rumour doth double, like the voice and echo, the numbers of the feared.

Please it your grace to go to bed.

Upon my soul, my lord, the powers that you already have sent forth shall bring this prize in very easily.

To comfort you the more, I have received a certain instance that Glendower is dead.

Your majesty hath been this fortnight ill and these unseasoned hours perforce must add unto your sickness.

King Henry IV

I will take your counsel, and were these inward wars once out of hand, we would, dear lords, unto the Holy Land.

(Exit)

Act 3 Scene 2

Gloucestershire. Before Shallow's house.

(Shallow and Silence enter, meeting; Mouldy, Shadow, Wart, Feeble, Bullcalf, a Servant or two with them

Shallow

Come on, come on, come on, sir; give me your hand, sir, give me your hand sir, an early stirrer by the rood!

And how doth my good cousin Silence?

Silence

Good morrow, good cousin Shallow.

Shallow

And how doth my cousin, your bedfellow?

And your fairest daughter and mine, my god-daughter Ellen?

Silence

Alas, a black housel, cousin Shallow!

Shallow

By yea and nay sir, I dare say my cousin William is become a good scholar, he is at Oxford still, is he not?

Silence

Indeed, sir, to my cost.

Shallow

A' must, then, to the inns of court shortly.

I was once of Clement's Inn, where I think they will talk of mad Shallow yet.

Silence

You were called lusty shallow then, cousin.

Shallow

By the mass, I was called anything

I would have done anything indeed too, and roundly too.

There was I, and little John Doit of Staffordshire, and black George Barnes, and Francis Pickbone, and

Will Squele a Cotswold man

You had not four such swinge-bucklers in all the inns of court again, and I may say to you, we knew where the bona-robas were and had the best of them all at commandment.

Then was Jack Falstaff, now Sir John, a boy, and page to Thomas Mowbray, Duke of Norfolk.

Silence

This Sir John, cousin, that comes hither anon about soldiers?

Shallow

The same Sir John, the very same. I see him break Skogan's head at the court-gate, when a' was a crack not thus high, and the very same day did I fight with one Sampson Stockfish, a fruiterer behind Gray's Inn.

Jesus, Jesus, the mad days that I have spent!

And to see how many of my old acquaintance are dead!

Silence

We shall all follow, cousin.

Shadow

Certain, it is certain

Very sure, very sure, death as the Psalmist saith, is certain to all

All shall die.

How a good yoke of bullocks at Stamford fair?

Silence

By my troth, I was not there.

Shallow

Death is certain.

Is old Double of your town living yet?

Silence

Dead, sir.

Shallow

Jesus, Jesus, dead! a' drew a good bow

And dead! a' shot a fine shoot, John a Gaunt loved him well, and betted much money on his head.

Dead! a' would have clapped in the clout at twelve score

Carried you a forehand shaft a fourteen and fourteen and a half, that it would have done a man's heart good to see.

How a score of ewes now?

Silence

Thereafter as they be, a score of good news may be worth ten pounds.

Shallow

And is old Double dead?

Silence

Here come two of Sir John Falstaff's men, as I think.

(Bardolph and one with him enter)

Bardolph

Good morrow, honest gentlemen, I beseech you, which is Justice Shallow?

Shallow

I am Robert Shallow, sir

A poor esquire of this county, and one of the king's justices of the peace, what is your good pleasure with me?

Bardolph

My captain, sir, commends him to you; my captain, Sir John Falstaff, a tall gentleman by heaven and a most gallant leader.

Shallow

He greets me well, sir. I knew him a good backsword man.

How doth the good knight?

May I ask how my lady his wife doth?

Bardolph

Sir, pardon

A soldier is better accommodated than with a wife.

Shallow

It is well said, in faith, sir; and it is well said indeed too.

Better accommodated! it is good

Yea indeed, is it, good phrases are surely and ever were very commendable.

Accommodated! it comes of 'accommodo' very good

A good phrase.

Bardolph

Pardon me, sir

I have heard the word.

Phrase call you it?

By this good day, I know not the phrase

I will maintain the word with my sword to be a soldier-like word, and a word of exceeding good command, by heaven.

Accommodated; that is, when a man is, as they say, accommodated

When a man is, being whereby as may be thought to be accommodated

Which is an excellent thing.

Shallow

It is very just.

(Falstaff enters)

Look, here comes good Sir John.

Give me your good hand, give me your worship's good hand, by my troth, you like well and bear your years very well, welcome, good Sir John.

Falstaff

I am glad to see you well, good Master Robert Shallow, Master Surecard, as I think?

Shallow

No, Sir John

It is my cousin Silence, in commission with me.

Falstaff

Good Master Silence, it well befits you should be of the peace.

Silence

Your good-worship is welcome.

Falstaff

Fie! this is hot weather, gentlemen.

Have you provided me here half a dozen sufficient men?

Shallow

Marry, have we, sir. Will you sit?

Falstaff

Let me see them, I beseech you.

Shallow

Where's the roll? Where's the roll?

Where's the roll? Let me see, let me see, let me see.

So, so, yea, marry, sir, Ralph Mouldy!

Let them appear as I call

Let them do so, let them do so.

Let me see

Where is Mouldy?

Mouldy

Here, and if it please you.

Shallow

What think you, Sir John? a good-limbed fellow

Young, strong, and of good friends

Falstaff

Is thy name Mouldy?

Mouldy

Yea, and if it please you.

Falstaff

It is the more time thou wert used.

Shallow

Ha, ha, ha! most excellent, in faith!

Things that are mouldy lack use, very singular good!

In faith, well said Sir John, very well said.

Falstaff

Prick him.

Mouldy

I was pricked well enough before, and you could have let me alone, my old dame will be undone now for one to do her husbandry and her drudgery, you need not to have pricked me

There are other men fitter to go out than I.

Falstaff

Go to

Peace Mouldy, you shall go.

Mouldy, it is time you were spent.

Mouldy

Spent!

Shallow

Peace, fellow, peace

Stand aside, know you where you are?

For the other, Sir John: let me see

Simon Shadow!

Falstaff

Yea, marry, let me have him to sit under, he's like to be a cold soldier.

Shallow

Where's Shadow?

Shadow

Here, sir.

Falstaff

Shadow, whose son art thou?

Shadow

My mother's son, sir.

Falstaff

Thy mother's son! like enough, and thy father's shadow, so the son of the female is the shadow of the male, it is often so, indeed

Much of the father's substance!

Shallow

Do you like him, Sir John?

Falstaff

Shadow will serve for summer

Prick him, for we have a number of shadows to fill up the muster-book.

Shallow

Thomas Wart!

Falstaff

Where's he?

Wart

Here, sir.

Falstaff

Is thy name Wart?

Wart

Yea, sir.

Falstaff

Thou art a very ragged wart.

Shallow

Shall I prick him down, Sir John?

Falstaff

It were superfluous; for his apparel is built upon his back and the whole frame stands upon pins, prick him no more.

Shallow

Ha, ha, ha! you can do it, sir; you can do it, I commend you well. Francis Feeble!

Feeble

Here, sir.

Falstaff

What trade art thou, Feeble?

Feeble

A woman's tailor, sir.

Shallow

Shall I prick him, sir?

Falstaff

You may: but if he had been a man's tailor, held have pricked you.

Wilt thou make as many holes in an enemy's battle as thou hast done in a woman's petticoat?

Feeble

I will do my good will, sir; you can have no more.

Falstaff

Well said, good woman's tailor! well said, courageous Feeble!

Thou wilt be as valiant as the wrathful dove or most magnanimous mouse.

Prick the woman's tailor, well Master Shallow

Deep Master Shallow.

Feeble

I would Wart might have gone, sir.

Falstaff

I would thou wert a man's tailor, that thou mightst mend him and make him fit to go.

I cannot put him to a private soldier that is the leader of so many thousands, let that suffice most forcible Feeble.

Feeble

It shall suffice, sir.

Falstaff

I am bound to thee, reverend Feeble.

Who is next?

Shallow

Peter Bullcalf of the green!

Falstaff

Yea, marry, let's see Bullcalf.

Bullcalf

Here, sir.

Falstaff

Before God, a likely fellow!

Come, prick me Bullcalf till he roar again.

Bullcalf

Oh Lord! good my lord captain...

Falstaff

What, dost thou roar before thou art pricked?

Bullcalf

Oh Lord, sir! I am a diseased man.

Falstaff

What disease hast thou?

Bullcalf

A whoreson cold, sir, a cough sir, which I caught with ringing in the king's affairs upon his coronation-day, sir.

Falstaff

Come, thou shalt go to the wars in a gown

We wilt have away thy cold; and I will take such order that my friends shall ring for thee.

Is here all?

Shallow

Here is two more called than your number, you must have but four here, sir, and so, I pray you, go in with me to dinner.

Falstaff

Come, I will go drink with you, but I cannot tarry dinner.

I am glad to see you, by my troth, Master Shallow.

Shallow

Oh Sir John, do you remember since we lay all night in the windmill in Saint George's field?

Falstaff

No more of that, good Master Shallow, no more of that.

Shallow

Ha! It was a merry night.

And is Jane Nightwork alive?

Falstaff

She lives, Master Shallow.

Shallow

She never could away with me.

Falstaff

Never, never; she would always say she could not abide Master Shallow.

Shallow

By the mass, I could anger her to the heart.

She was then a bona-roba.

Doth she hold her own well?

Falstaff

Old, old, Master Shallow

Shallow

Nay, she must be old; she cannot choose but be old

Certain she's old

Had Robin Nightwork by old Nightwork before I came to Clement's Inn.

Silence

That's fifty-five year ago.

Shallow

Ha, cousin Silence, that thou hadst seen that that this knight and I have seen!

Ha, Sir John, said I well?

Falstaff

We have heard the chimes at midnight, Master Shallow.

Shallow

That we have, that we have, that we have

In faith, Sir John, we have, our watch-word was Hem boys!

Come, let's to dinner

Come, let's to dinner

Jesus, the days that we have seen!

Come, come.

(Falstaff and Justices exit)

Bullcalf

Good Master Corporate Bardolph, stand my friend

Here's four Harry ten shillings in French crowns for you.

In very truth, sir, I had as lief be hanged sir, as go, and yet for mine own part, sir I do not care

Rather, because I am unwilling and, for mine own part have a desire to stay with my friends

Else sir, I did not care, for mine own part, so much.

Bardolph

Go to

Stand aside.

Mouldy

And, good master corporal captain, for my old dame's sake, stand my friend, she has nobody to do anything about her when I am gone

She is old and cannot help herself, you shall have forty, sir.

Bardolph

Go to.

Stand aside.

Feeble

By my troth, I care not

A man can die but once, we owe God a death, I'll never bear a base mind, and it be my destiny so

And it be not, so no man is too good to serve's prince

Let it go which way it will, he that dies this year is quit for the next.

Bardolph

Well said

Thou'rt a good fellow.

Feeble

Faith, I'll bear no base mind.

(Falstaff and the Justices re-enter)

Falstaff

Come, sir, which men shall I have?

Shallow

Four of which you please.

Bardolph

Sir, a word with you, I have three pound to free Mouldy and Bullcalf.

Falstaff

Go to

Well.

Shallow

Come, Sir John, which four will you have?

Falstaff

Do you choose for me.

Shallow

Marry, then, Mouldy, Bullcalf, Feeble and Shadow.

Falstaff

Mouldy and Bullcalf, for you Mouldy, stay at home till you are past service, and for your part Bullcalf, grow till you come unto it, I will none of you.

Shallow

Sir John, Sir John, do not yourself wrong, they are your likeliest men and I would have you served with the best.

Falstaff

Will you tell me, Master Shallow, how to choose a man?

Care I for the limb, the thighs, the stature, bulk, and big assemblance of a man!

Give me the spirit, Master Shallow.

Here's Wart; you see what a ragged appearance it is

A' shall charge you and discharge you with the motion of a pewterer's hammer, come off and on swifter than he that gibbets on the brewer's bucket.

This same half-faced fellow, Shadow

Give me this man: he presents no mark to the enemy

The foeman may with as great aim level at the edge of a penknife.

And for a retreat

How swiftly will this feeble, the woman's tailor run

off!

Oh give me the spare men, and spare me the great ones.

Put me a cleaver into Wart's hand, Bardolph.

Bardolph

Hold, Wart, traverse; thus, thus, thus.

Falstaff

Come, manage me your caliver.

So, very well, go to, very good, exceeding good.

Oh give me always a little, lean, old, chapt bald shot.

Well said, in good faith, Wart

Thou'rt a good scab, hold, there's a tester for thee.

Shallow

He is not his craft's master; he doth not do it right.

I remember at Mile-end Green, when I lay at Clement's Inn…

I was then Sir Dagonet in Arthur's show…

There was a little quiver fellow, and a' would manage you his piece thus; and a' would about and about, and come you in and come you in, 'rah, tah, tah, would a say Bounce would a say

Away again would a' go, and again would a' come, I shall never see such a fellow.

Falstaff

These fellows will do well, Master Shallow.

God keep you, Master Silence, I will not use many words with you.

Fare you well, gentlemen both, I thank you, I must a dozen mile tonight. Bardolph, give the soldiers coats.

Shallow

Sir John, the Lord bless you! God prosper your affairs! God send us peace!

At your return visit our house

Let our old acquaintance be renewed

Peradventure I will with ye to the court.

Falstaff

Before God, I would you would, Master Shallow.

Shallow

Go to

I have spoke at a word. God keep you.

Falstaff

Fare you well, gentle gentlemen.

(Justices exit)

On, Bardolph

Lead the men away.

(Bardolph, Recruits, & company exit)

As I return, I will fetch off these justices, I do see the bottom of Justice Shallow.

Lord, Lord, how subject we old men are to this vice of lying!

This same starved justice hath done nothing but prate to me of the wildness of his youth, and the feats he hath done about Turnbull Street: and every third word a lie, duer paid to the hearer than the Turk's tribute.

I do remember him at Clement's Inn like a man made after supper of a cheese-paring

When a' was naked, he was for all the world like a forked radish, with a head fantastically carved upon it with a knife

A' was so forlorn, that his dimensions to any thick sight were invincible, a' was the very genius of famine

Yet lecherous as a monkey, and the whores called him mandrake, a' came ever in the rearward of the fashion, and sung those tunes to the overscutched huswives that he heard the carmen whistle and swear they were his fancies or his good-nights.

And now is this Vice's dagger become a squire, and talks as familiarly of John a Gaunt as if he had been sworn brother to him

I'll be sworn a' ne'er saw him but once in the tilt-yard; and then he burst his head for crowding among the marshal's men.

I saw it, and told John a Gaunt he beat his own name; for you might have thrust him and all his apparel into an eel-skin

The case of a treble hautboy was a mansion for him, a court, and now has he land and beefs.

Well, I'll be acquainted with him, if I return it shall go hard but I will make him a philosopher's two stones to me, if the young dace be a bait for the old pike, I see no reason in the law of nature but I may snap at him. Let time shape, and there an end.

(Exits)

Act 4 Scene 1

Yorkshire. Gaultree Forest.

(The Archbishop of York, Mowbray, Lord Hastings, and others enter)

Archbishop of York

What is this forest called?

Hastings

It is Gaultree Forest, and it shall please your grace.

Archbishop of York

Here stand, my lords; and send discoverers forth to know the numbers of our enemies.

Hastings

We have sent forth already.

Archbishop of York

It is well done.

My friends and brethren in these great affairs,

I must acquaint you that I have received new-dated letters from Northumberland

Their cold intent, tenor and substance, thus here doth he wish his person, with such powers as might hold sortance with his quality, the which he could not levy

Whereupon he is retired to ripe his growing fortunes to Scotland, and concludes in hearty prayers that your attempts may overlive the hazard and fearful melting of their opposite.

Mowbray

Thus do the hopes we have in him touch ground and dash themselves to pieces.

(A Messenger enters)

Hastings

Now, what news?

Messenger

West of this forest, scarcely off a mile in goodly form comes on the enemy

By the ground they hide, I judge their number upon or near the rate of thirty thousand.

Mowbray

The just proportion that we gave them out, let us sway on and face them in the field.

Archbishop of York

What well-appointed leader fronts us here?

(Westmoreland enters)

Mowbray

I think it is my Lord of Westmoreland.

Westmoreland

Health and fair greeting from our general, the prince, Lord John and Duke of Lancaster.

Archbishop of York

Say on, my Lord of Westmoreland, in peace

What doth concern your coming?

Westmoreland

Then, my lord, unto your grace do I in chief address the substance of my speech.

If that rebellion came like itself, in base and abject routs, led on by bloody youth, guarded with rags, and countenanced by boys and beggary I say, if damned commotion so appeared in his true native and most proper shape

You, reverend father, and these noble lords had not been here to dress the ugly form of base and bloody insurrection with your fair honours.

You, lord archbishop, whose see is by a civil peace maintained, whose beard the silver hand of peace hath touched, whose learning and good letters peace hath tutored, whose white investments figure innocence, the dove and very blessed spirit of peace,

Wherefore do you so ill translate ourself out of the speech of peace that bears such grace into the harsh and boisterous tongue of war

Turning your books to graves, your ink to blood, your pens to lances and your tongue divine, to a trumpet and a point of war?

Archbishop of York

Wherefore do I this? so the question stands.

Briefly to this end, we are all diseased, and with our surfeiting and wanton hours have brought ourselves into a burning fever, and we must bleed for it; of which disease our late king, Richard, being infected, died.

But, my most noble Lord of Westmoreland, I take not on me here as a physician, nor do I troop in the throngs of military men as an enemy to peace

But rather show awhile like fearful war, to diet rank minds sick of happiness and purge the obstructions which begin to stop our very veins of life.

Hear me more plainly.

I have in equal balance justly weighed what wrongs our arms may do, what wrongs we suffer, and find our griefs heavier than our offences.

We see which way the stream of time doth run, and are enforced from our most quiet there by the rough torrent of occasion

And have the summary of all our griefs, when time shall serve to show in articles

Which long were this we offered to the king, and might by no suit gain our audience, when we are wronged and would unfold our griefs, we are denied access unto his person even by those men that most have done us wrong.

The dangers of the days but newly gone, whose memory is written on the earth with yet appearing blood, and the examples of every minute's instance, present now hath put us in these ill-beseeming arms, not to break peace or any branch of it, but to establish here a peace indeed, concurring both in name and quality.

Westmoreland

When ever yet was your appeal denied?

Wherein have you been galled by the king?

What peer hath been suborn'd to grate on you, that you should seal this lawless bloody book of forged rebellion with a seal divine and consecrate commotion's bitter edge?

Archbishop of York

My brother general, the commonwealth to brother born an household cruelty, I make my quarrel in particular.

Westmoreland

There is no need of any such redress

Or if there were, it not belongs to you.

Mowbray

Why not to him in part, and to us all that feel the bruises of the days before and suffer the condition of these times to lay a heavy and unequal hand upon our honours?

Westmoreland

Oh my good Lord Mowbray, construe the times to their necessities and you shall say indeed, it is the time, and not the king that doth you injuries.

Yet for your part, it not appears to me either from the king or in the present time that you should have an inch of any ground to build a grief on

Were you not restored to all the Duke of Norfolk's signories, your noble and right well remembered father's?

Mowbray

What thing, in honour, had my father lost, that need to be revived and breathed in me?

The king that loved him, as the state stood then was force perforce compelled to banish him, and then that Harry Bolingbroke and he, being mounted and both roused in their seats,

Their neighing coursers daring of the spur, their armed staves in charge, their beavers down, their eyes of fire sparking through sights of steel and the loud trumpet blowing them together

Then, then, when there was nothing could have stayed my father from the breast of Bolingbroke, oh when the king did throw his warder down, his own life hung upon the staff he threw

Then threw he down himself and all their lives that by indictment and by dint of sword have since miscarried under Bolingbroke.

Westmoreland

You speak, Lord Mowbray, now you know not what

The Earl of Hereford was reputed then in England the most valiant gentlemen, who knows on whom fortune would then have smiled?

But if your father had been victor there, he ne'er had borne it out of Coventry, for all the country in a general voice cried hate upon him; and all their prayers and love were set on Hereford, whom they doted on and blessed and graced indeed, more than the king.

But this is mere digression from my purpose.

Here come I from our princely general to know your griefs; to tell you from his grace that he will give you audience

Wherein it shall appear that your demands are just, you shall enjoy them, everything set off that might so much as think you enemies.

Mowbray

But he hath forced us to compel this offer

It proceeds from policy, not love.

Westmoreland

Mowbray, you overween to take it so

This offer comes from mercy, not from fear, for lord!

Within a ken our army lies, upon mine honour, all too confident to give admittance to a thought of fear.

Our battle is more full of names than yours, our men more perfect in the use of arms, our armour all as strong, our cause the best

Then reason will our heart should be as good say you not then our offer is compelled.

Mowbray

Well, by my will we shall admit no parley.

Westmoreland

That argues but the shame of your offence, a rotten case abides no handling.

Hastings

Hath the Prince John a full commission, in very ample virtue of his father, to hear and absolutely to determine

Of what conditions we shall stand upon?

Westmoreland

That is intended in the general's name, I muse you make so slight a question.

Archbishop of York

Then take, my Lord of Westmoreland, this schedule, for this contains our general grievances, each several article herein redressed, all members of our cause, both here and hence that are insinewed to this action

Acquitted by a true substantial form and present execution of our wills to us and to our purposes confined, we come within our awful banks again and knit our powers to the arm of peace.

Westmoreland

This will I show the general.

Please you, lords, in sight of both our battles we may meet

Either end in peace, which God so frame!

Or to the place of difference call the swords which must decide it.

Archbishop of York

My lord, we will do so.

(Westmoreland exits)

Mowbray

There is a thing within my bosom tells me that no conditions of our peace can stand.

Hastings

Fear you not that: if we can make our peace upon such large terms and so absolute as our conditions shall consist upon, our peace shall stand as firm as rocky mountains.

Mowbray

Yea, but our valuation shall be such that every slight and false-derived cause, yea, every idle nice and wanton reason shall to the king taste of this action

That, were our royal faiths martyrs in love, we shall be winnowed with so rough a wind that even our corn shall seem as light as chaff and good from bad find no partition.

Archbishop of York

No, no, my lord. Note this; the king is weary of dainty and such picking grievances, for he hath found to end one doubt by death revives two greater in the heirs of life, and therefore will he wipe his tables clean and keep no tell-tale to his memory that may repeat and history his loss to new remembrance

For full well he knows he cannot so precisely weed this land as his misdoubts present occasion, his foes are so enrooted with his friends that, plucking to unfix an enemy

He doth unfasten so and shake a friend, so that this land, like an offensive wife that hath enraged him on to offer strokes, as he is striking, holds his infant up and hangs resolved correction in the arm that was upreared to execution.

Hastings

Besides, the king hath wasted all his rods on late offenders, that he now doth lack the very instruments of chastisement, so that his power, like to a fangless lion, may offer but not hold.

Archbishop of York

It is very true, and therefore be assured, my good lord marshal, if we do now make our atonement well

Our peace will, like a broken limb united, grow stronger for the breaking.

Mowbray

Be it so.

Here is returned my Lord of Westmoreland.

(Westmoreland re-enters)

Westmoreland

The prince is here at hand, pleaseth your lordship to meet his grace just distance 'tween our armies.

Mowbray

Your grace of York, in God's name then, set forward.

Archbishop of York

Before, and greet his grace: my lord, we come.

(Exit)

Act 4 Scene 2

Another part of the forest.

(Mowbray enters attended from one side, afterwards the Archbishop of York, Hastings, and others enter from the other side with Prince John of Lancaster, and Westmoreland, Officers, and others with them)

Lancaster

You are well encountered here, my cousin Mowbray, Good day to you, gentle lord archbishop

And so to you, Lord Hastings, and to all

My Lord of York, it better showed with you when that your flock, assembled by the bell, encircled you to hear with reverence your exposition on the holy text than now to see you here an iron man cheering a rout of rebels with your drum,

Turning the word to sword and life to death.

That man that sits within a monarch's heart and ripens in the sunshine of his favour would he abuse the countenance of the king

Alas, what mischiefs might he set abrooch, in shadow of such greatness!

With you, lord bishop, it is even so.

Who hath not heard it spoken how deep you were within the books of God?

To us the speaker in his parliament

To us the imagined voice of God himself

The very opener and intelligencer between the grace, the sanctities of heaven and our dull workings

Oh who shall believe but you misuse the reverence of your place, employ the countenance and grace of heaven as a false favourite doth his prince's name,

In deeds dishonourable? You have taken up under the counterfeited zeal of God, the subjects of his substitute, my father and both against the peace of heaven and him have here up-swarmed them.

Archbishop of York

Good my Lord of Lancaster, I am not here against your father's peace

As I told my lord of Westmoreland, the time misordered doth, in common sense, crowd us and crush us to this monstrous form to hold our safety up.

I sent your grace the parcels and particulars of our grief, the which hath been with scorn shoved from the court whereon this Hydra son of war is born

Whose dangerous eyes may well be charmed asleep with grant of our most just and right desires, and true obedience of this madness cured, stoop tamely to the foot of majesty.

Mowbray

If not, we ready are to try our fortunes to the last man.

Hastings

And though we here fall down, we have supplies to second our attempt, if they miscarry, theirs shall second them

And so success of mischief shall be born and heir from heir shall hold this quarrel up whiles England shall have generation.

Lancaster

You are too shallow, Hastings, much too shallow, to sound the bottom of the after-times.

Westmoreland

Pleaseth your grace to answer them directly how far forth you do like their articles.

Lancaster

I like them all, and do allow them well and swear here, by the honour of my blood, my father's purposes have been mistook and some about him have too lavishly wrested his meaning and authority.

My lord, these griefs shall be with speed redressed

Upon my soul, they shall. If this may please you, discharge your powers unto their several counties, as we will ours, and here between the armies.

Let's drink together friendly and embrace that all their eyes may bear those tokens home of our restored love and amity.

Archbishop of York

I take your princely word for these redresses.

Lancaster

I give it you, and will maintain my word and thereupon I drink unto your grace.

Hastings

Go, captain, and deliver to the army this news of peace, let them have pay and part, I know it will well please them.

Hie thee, captain.

(Officer exits)

Archbishop of York

To you, my noble Lord of Westmoreland.

Westmoreland

I pledge your grace; and, if you knew what pains I have bestowed to breed this present peace, you would drink freely, but my love to ye shall show itself more openly hereafter.

Archbishop of York

I do not doubt you.

Westmoreland

I am glad of it.

Health to my lord and gentle cousin, Mowbray.

Mowbray

You wish me health in very happy season

For I am, on the sudden, something ill.

Archbishop of York

Against ill chances men are ever merry

But heaviness foreruns the good event.

Westmoreland

Therefore be merry, coz; since sudden sorrow serves to say thus, some good thing comes to-morrow.

Archbishop of York

Believe me, I am passing light in spirit.

Mowbray

So much the worse, if your own rule be true.

(Shouts within)

Lancaster

The word of peace is rendered, hark, how they shout!

Mowbray

This had been cheerful after victory.

Archbishop of York

A peace is of the nature of a conquest

For then both parties nobly are subdued and neither party loser.

Lancaster

Go, my lord, and let our army be discharged too.

(Exits) Westmoreland

And, good my lord, so please you, let our trains march, by us, that we may peruse the men we should have coped withal.

Archbishop of York

Go good Lord Hastings, and here they be dismissed, let them march by.

(Hastings exits)

Lancaster

I trust, lords, we shall lie to-night together.

(Westmoreland re-enters)

Now, cousin, wherefore stands our army still?

Westmoreland

The leaders, having charge from you to stand, will not go off until they hear you speak.

Lancaster

They know their duties.

(Hastings re-enters)

Hastings

My lord, our army is dispersed already

Like youthful steers unyoked, they take their courses east, west, north, south

Like a school broke up, each hurries toward his home and sporting-place.

Westmoreland

Good tidings, my Lord Hastings

The which I do arrest thee, traitor, of high treason, and you, lord archbishop, and you Lord Mowbray, of capitol treason I attach you both.

Mowbray

Is this proceeding just and honourable?

Westmoreland

Is your assembly so?

Archbishop of York

Will you thus break your faith?

Lancaster

I pawned thee none, I promised you redress of these same grievances whereof you did complain

Which, by mine honour, I will perform with a most Christian care

But for you, rebels, look to taste the due meet for rebellion and such acts as yours.

Most shallowly did you these arms commence, fondly brought here and foolishly sent hence.

Strike up our drums, pursue the scattered stray, God, and not we, hath safely fought to-day.

Some guard these traitors to the block of death, Treason's true bed and yielder up of breath.

(Exit)

Act 4 Scene 3

Another part of the forest.

Alarum. Excursions.

(Falstaff and Colevile enter, meeting)

Falstaff

What's your name, sir? of what condition are you and of what place, I pray?

Colevile

I am a knight, sir, and my name is Colevile of the dale.

Falstaff

Well, then, Colevile is your name, a knight is your degree and your place the dale, Colevile shall be still your name, a traitor your degree, and the dungeon your place, a place deep enough

So shall you be still Colevile of the dale.

Colevile

Are not you Sir John Falstaff?

Falstaff

As good a man as he, sir, whoe'er I am.

Do ye yield, sir? or shall I sweat for you?

If I do sweat, they are the drops of thy lovers, and they weep for thy death, therefore rouse up fear and trembling, and do observance to my mercy.

Colevile

I think you are Sir John Falstaff, and in that thought yield me.

Falstaff

I have a whole school of tongues in this belly of mine, and not a tongue of them all speaks any other word but my name.

And I had but a belly of any indifference, I were simply the most active fellow in Europe, my womb, my womb, my womb, undoes me.

Here comes our general.

(Prince John of Lancaster, Westmoreland, Blunt, and others enter)

Lancaster

The heat is past; follow no further now:

Call in the powers, good cousin Westmoreland.

(Westmoreland exits)

Now, Falstaff, where have you been all this while?

When everything is ended, then you come, these tardy tricks of yours will on my life, one time or other break some gallows' back.

Falstaff

I would be sorry, my lord, but it should be thus, I never knew yet but rebuke and cheque was the reward of valour.

Do you think me a swallow, an arrow, or a bullet?

Have I, in my poor and old motion, the expedition of thought?

I have speeded hither with the very extremest inch of possibility

I have foundered nine score and odd posts, and here, travel-tainted as I am, have in my pure and immaculate valour, taken Sir John Colevile of the dale, a most furious knight and valorous enemy.

But what of that? he saw me, and yielded; that I may justly say, with the hook-nosed fellow of Rome, I came, saw, and overcame.

Lancaster

It was more of his courtesy than your deserving.

Falstaff

I know not: here he is, and here I yield him, and

I beseech your grace, let it be booked with the rest of this day's deeds

By the Lord, I will have it in a particular ballad else, with mine own picture on the top on it, Colevile kissing my foot

To the which course if I be enforced, if you do not all show like gilt two pences to me, and I in the clear sky of fame overshine you as much as the full moon doth the cinders of the element, which show like pins' heads to her, believe not the word of the noble, therefore let me have right, and let desert mount.

Lancaster

Thine's too heavy to mount.

Falstaff

Let it shine, then.

Lancaster

Thine's too thick to shine.

Falstaff

Let it do something, my good lord, that may do me good, and call it what you will.

Lancaster

Is thy name Colevile?

Colevile

It is, my lord.

Lancaster

A famous rebel art thou, Colevile.

Falstaff

And a famous true subject took him.

Colevile

I am, my lord, but as my betters are that led me hither: had they been ruled by me, you should have won them dearer than you have.

Falstaff

I know not how they sold themselves, but thou like a kind fellow, gavest thyself away gratis

I thank thee for thee.

(Westmoreland re-enters)

Lancaster

Now, have you left pursuit?

Westmoreland

Retreat is made and execution stay'd.

Lancaster

Send Colevile with his confederates to York, to present execution, blunt, lead him hence

See you guard him sure.

(Blunt and others exit with Colevile)

And now dispatch we toward the court, my lords, I hear the king my father is sore sick, our news shall go before us to his majesty, which, cousin, you shall bear to comfort him and we with sober speed will follow you.

Falstaff

My lord, I beseech you, give me leave to go through Gloucestershire, and when you come to court, stand my good lord, pray, in your good report.

Lancaster

Fare you well, Falstaff, I, in my condition shall better speak of you than you deserve.

(All but Falstaff exit)

Falstaff

I would you had but the wit: 'twere better than your dukedom.

Good faith, this same young sober-blooded boy doth not love me

A man cannot make him laugh

That's no marvel, he drinks no wine

There's never none of these demure boys come to any proof

Thin drink doth so over-cool their blood, and making many fish-meals, that they fall into a kind of male green-sickness; and then when they marry, they get wenches, they are generally fools and cowards

Some of us should be too, but for inflammation.

A good sherris sack hath a two-fold operation in it. It ascends me into the brain

Dries me there all the foolish and dull and curdy vapours which environ it; makes it apprehensive, quick, forgetive, full of nimble fiery and delectable shapes, which, delivered over to the voice the tongue, which is the birth, becomes excellent wit.

The second property of your excellent sherris is, the warming of the blood

Before cold and settled, left the liver white and pale, which is the badge of pusillanimity and cowardice

The sherris warms it and makes it course from the inwards to the parts extreme, it illumineth the face, which as a beacon gives warning to all the rest of this little kingdom, man, to arm

Then the vital commoners and inland petty spirits muster me all to their captain, the heart, who, great and puffed up with this retinue doth any deed of courage

This valour comes of sherris.

So that skill in the weapon is nothing without sack, for that sets it a-work

Learning a mere hoard of gold kept by a devil, till sack commences it and sets it in act and use.

Hereof comes it that Prince Harry is valiant

For the cold blood he did naturally inherit of his father, he hath, like lean, sterile and bare land, manured, husbanded and tilled with excellent endeavour of drinking good and good store of fertile sherris, that he is become very hot and valiant.

If I had a thousand sons, the first humane principle I

would teach them should be, to forswear thin potations and to addict themselves to sack.

(Bardolph enters)

How now Bardolph?

Bardolph

The army is discharged all and gone.

Falstaff

Let them go.

I'll through Gloucestershire

There will I visit Master Robert Shallow esquire, I have him already tempering between my finger and my thumb, and shortly will I seal with him.

Come away.

(Exit)

Act 4 Scene 4

Westminster. The Jerusalem Chamber.

(King Henry IV, the Princes Thomas of Clarence and Humphrey of Gloucester, Warkwick, and others enter)

King Henry IV
Now, lords, if God doth give successful end to this debate that bleedeth at our doors, we will our youth lead on to higher fields and draw no swords but what are sanctified.
Our navy is addressed, our power collected, uur substitutes in absence well invested and everything lies level to our wish
We want a little personal strength, pause us till these rebels, now afoot, come underneath the yoke of government.

Warkwick
Both which we doubt not but your majesty shall soon enjoy.

King Henry IV
Humphrey, my son of Gloucester, where is the prince your brother?

Gloucester
I think he's gone to hunt, my lord, at Windsor.

King Henry IV

And how accompanied?

Gloucester

I do not know, my lord.

King Henry IV

Is not his brother, Thomas of Clarence, with him?

Gloucester

No, my good lord He is in presence here.

Clarence

What would my lord and father?

King Henry IV

Nothing but well to thee, Thomas of Clarence.

How chance thou art not with the prince thy brother?

He loves thee, and thou dost neglect him, Thomas

Thou hast a better place in his affection than all thy brothers,

cherish it my boy, and noble offices thou mayst effect of

mediation, after I am dead between his greatness and thy

other brethren

Therefore omit him not, blunt not his love, nor lose the good advantage of his grace by seeming cold or careless of his will
For he is gracious, if he be observed, he hath a tear for pity and a hand open as day for melting charity
Yet notwithstanding, being incensed, he's flint, as humorous as winter and as sudden as flaws congealed in the spring of day.
His temper, therefore, must be well observed, chide him for faults, and do it reverently, when thou perceive his blood inclined to mirth
Being moody, give him line and scope, till that his passions, like a whale on ground, confound themselves with working.
Learn this, Thomas, and thou shalt prove a shelter to thy friends, a hoop of gold to bind thy brothers in that the united vessel of their blood mingled with venom of suggestion…
As, force perforce, the age will pour it in…
Shall never leak, though it do work as strong as aconitum or rash gunpowder.

Clarence

I shall observe him with all care and love.

King Henry IV

Why art thou not at Windsor with him, Thomas?

Clarence He is not there to-day

He dines in London.

King Henry IV

And how accompanied? canst thou tell that?

Clarence

With Poins, and other his continual followers.

King Henry IV

Most subject is the fattest soil to weeds

The noble image of my youth is overspread with them,

therefore my grief stretches itself beyond the hour of death

The blood weeps from my heart when I do shape in forms

imaginary the unguided days and rotten times that you shall

look upon, when I am sleeping with my ancestors.

For when his headstrong riot hath no curb when rage and hot

blood are his counsellors, when means and lavish manners

meet together, oh with what wings shall his affections fly

towards fronting peril and opposed decay!

Warkwick

My gracious lord, you look beyond him quite, the prince but

studies his companions like a strange tongue, wherein, to gain

the language, it is needful that the most immodest word be

looked upon and learned

Once attained your highness knows, comes to no further use

but to be known and hated.

So, like gross terms, the prince will in the perfectness of time

cast off his followers

Their memory shall as a pattern or a measure live, by which his grace must meet the lives of others, turning past evils to advantages.

King Henry IV

It is seldom when the bee doth leave her comb in the dead carrion.

(Westmoreland enters)

Who's here? Westmoreland?

Westmoreland

Health to my sovereign, and new happiness added to that that I am to deliver!

Prince John your son doth kiss your grace's hand, Mowbray, the Bishop Scroop, Hastings and all are brought to the correction of your law

There is not now a rebel's sword unsheathed, but peace puts forth her olive everywhere.

The manner how this action hath been borne here at more leisure may your highness read, with every course in his particular.

King Henry IV

Oh Westmoreland, thou art a summer bird, which ever in the haunch of winter sings the lifting up of day.

(Harcourt enters)

Look, here's more news.

Harcourt

From enemies heaven keep your majesty

When they stand against you, may they fall as those that I am come to tell you of!

The Earl Northumberland and the Lord Bardolph, with a great power of English and of Scots are by the sheriff of Yorkshire overthrown, the manner and true order of the fight this packet, please it you, contains at large.

King Henry IV

And wherefore should these good news make me sick?

Will fortune never come with both hands full, but write her fair words still in foulest letters?

She either gives a stomach and no food

Such are the poor, in health; or else a feast and takes away the stomach; such are the rich that have abundance and enjoy it not.

I should rejoice now at this happy news

And now my sight fails, and my brain is giddy, oh me!

Come near me

Now I am much ill.

Gloucester

Comfort, your majesty!

Clarence

Oh my royal father!

Westmoreland

My sovereign lord, cheer up yourself, look up.

Warkwick

Be patient, princes

You do know, these fits are with his highness very ordinary. Stand from him.

Give him air

He'll straight be well.

Clarence

No, no, he cannot long hold out these pangs, the incessant care and labour of his mind hath wrought the mure that should confine it in so thin that life looks through and will break out.

Gloucester

The people fear me; for they do observe unfathered heirs and loathly births of nature, the seasons change their manners, as the year had found some months asleep and leaped them over.

Clarence

The river hath thrice flowed, no web between The old folk, time's doting chronicles, say it did so a little time before that our great-grandsire, Edward, sicked and died.

Warkwick

Speak lower, princes, for the king recovers.

Gloucester

This apoplexy will certain be his end.

King Henry IV

I pray you, take me up, and bear me hence into some other chamber: softly, pray.

Act 4 Scene 5

Another chamber.

(King Henry IV lying on a bed, Clarence, Gloucester, Warkwick, and others in attendance)

King Henry IV

Let there be no noise made, my gentle friends

Unless some dull and favourable hand will whisper music to my weary spirit

Warkwick

Call for the music in the other room.

King Henry IV

Set me the crown upon my pillow here.

Clarence

His eye is hollow, and he changes much.

Warkwick

Less noise, less noise!

(Prince Henry)

Prince Henry

Who saw the Duke of Clarence?

Clarence

I am here, brother, full of heaviness.

Prince Henry

How now! rain within doors, and none abroad!

How doth the king?

Gloucester

Exceeding ill.

Prince Henry

Heard he the good news yet?

Tell it him.

Gloucester

He altered much upon the hearing it.

Prince Henry

If he be sick with joy, he'll recover without physic.

Warkwick

Not so much noise, my lords, sweet prince, speak low

The king your father is disposed to sleep.

Clarence

Let us withdraw into the other room.

Warkwick

Will it please your grace to go along with us?

Prince Henry

No; I will sit and watch here by the king.

(All but Prince Henry exit)

Why doth the crown lie there upon his pillow, being so troublesome a bedfellow?

Oh polished perturbation! golden care!

That keep'st the ports of slumber open wide to many a watchful night! sleep with it now!

Yet not so sound and half so deeply sweet as he whose brow with homely biggen bound snores out the watch of night.

Oh majesty!

When thou dost pinch thy bearer, thou dost sit like a rich armour worn in heat of day, that scalds with safety.

By his gates of breath there lies a downy feather which stirs not, did he suspire, that light and weightless down perforce must move.

My gracious lord! my father!

This sleep is sound indeed, this is a sleep that from this golden rigol hath divorced so many English kings.

Thy due from me is tears and heavy sorrows of the blood, which nature, love, and filial tenderness, shall, oh dear father pay thee plenteously

My due from thee is this imperial crown, which as immediate as thy place and blood, derives itself to me. Lord, here it sits which God shall guard

Put the world's whole strength into one giant arm, it shall not force this lineal honour from me: this from thee will I to mine leave, as it is left to me.

(Exits)

King Henry IV

Warwick! Gloucester! Clarence!

(Warkwick, Gloucester, Clarence, and the rest re-enter)

Clarence

Doth the king call?

Warkwick

What would your majesty? How fares your grace?

King Henry IV

Why did you leave me here alone, my lords?

Clarence

We left the prince my brother here, my liege who undertook to sit and watch by you.

King Henry IV

The Prince of Wales! Where is he? let me see him, he is not here.

Warkwick

This door is open; he is gone this way.

Gloucester

He came not through the chamber where we stay'd.

King Henry IV

Where is the crown? who took it from my pillow?

Warkwick

When we withdrew, my liege, we left it here.

King Henry IV

The prince hath taken it hence: go, seek him out.

Is he so hasty that he doth suppose my sleep my death?

Find him, my Lord of Warwick; chide him hither.

(Warkwick exits)

This part of his conjoins with my disease and helps to end me.

See, sons, what things you are!

How quickly nature falls into revolt when gold becomes her object!

For this the foolish over-careful fathers have broke their sleep with thoughts, their brains with care, their bones with industry

For this they have engrossed and piled up the cankered heaps of strange-achieved gold

For this they have been thoughtful to invest their sons with arts and martial exercises, when like the bee, culling from every flower the virtuous sweets, our thighs packed with wax, our mouths with honey, we bring it to the hive, and like the bees are murdered for our pains.

This bitter taste yield his engrossments to the ending father.

(Warkwick re-enters)

Now, where is he that will not stay so long till his friend sickness hath determined me?

Warkwick

My lord, I found the prince in the next room washing with kindly tears his gentle cheeks, with such a deep demeanor in great sorrow that tyranny, which never quaffed but blood, would by beholding him have washwd his knife with gentle eye-drops.

He is coming hither.

King Henry IV

But wherefore did he take away the crown?

(Prince Henry re-enters)

Lord, here he comes.

Come hither to me, Harry.

Depart the chamber, leave us here alone.

(Warkwick and the rest exit)

Prince Henry

I never thought to hear you speak again.

King Henry IV

Thy wish was father, Harry, to that thought, I stay too long by thee, I weary thee.

Dost thou so hunger for mine empty chair that thou wilt needs invest thee with my honours before thy hour be ripe?

Oh foolish youth! Thou seek'st the greatness that will overwhelm thee.

Stay but a little; for my cloud of dignity is held from falling with so weak a wind that it will quickly drop, my day is dim.

Thou hast stolen that which after some few hours were thine without offence

At my death thou hast sealed up my expectation, thy life did manifest thou lovedst me not and thou wilt have me die assured of it.

Thou hidest a thousand daggers in thy thoughts, which thou hast whetted on thy stony heart to stab at half an hour of my life.

What! canst thou not forbear me half an hour?

Then get thee gone and dig my grave thyself and bid the merry bells ring to thine ear that thou art crowned, not that I am dead.

Let all the tears that should bedew my hearse be drops of balm to sanctify thy head, only compound me with forgotten dust give that which gave thee life unto the worms.

Pluck down my officers, break my decrees

For now a time is come to mock at form, Harry the Fifth is crowned, up, vanity!

Down, royal state! all you sage counsellors, hence!

And to the English court assemble now, from every region, apes of idleness!

Now, neighbour confines, purge you of your scum have you a ruffian that will swear, drink, dance, revel the night, rob, murder, and commit the oldest sins the newest kind of ways?

Be happy, he will trouble you no more

England shall double gild his treble guilt, England shall give him office, honour, might

For the fifth Harry from curbed licence plucks the muzzle of restraint, and the wild dog shall flesh his tooth on every innocent.

Oh my poor kingdom, sick with civil blows!

When that my care could not withhold thy riots, what wilt thou do when riot is thy care?

Oh thou wilt be a wilderness again, peopled with wolves, thy old inhabitants!

Prince Henry

Oh pardon me, my liege! but for my tears, the moist impediments unto my speech, I had forestalled this dear and deep rebuke here you with grief had spoke and I had heard the course of it so far.

There is your crown

He that wears the crown immortally long guard it yours!

If I affect it more than as your honour and as your renown, let me no more from this obedience rise, which my most inward true and duteous spirit teacheth, this prostrate and exterior bending.

God witness with me, when I here came in and found no course of breath within your majesty, how cold it struck my heart! If I do feign, oh let me in my present wildness die and never live to show the incredulous world the noble change that I have purposed!

Coming to look on you, thinking you dead, and dead almost my liege, to think you were, I spake unto this crown as having sense and thus upbraided it

The care on thee depending hath fed upon the body of my father

Therefore, thou best of gold art worst of gold, other less fine in carat is more precious, preserving life in medicine potable

But thou, most fine, most honoured, most renowned hast eat thy bearer up.

Thus, my most royal liege, accusing it, I put it on my head to try with it, as with an enemy that had before my face murdered my father, the quarrel of a true inheritor.

But if it did infect my blood with joy, or swell my thoughts to any strain of pride, if any rebel or vain spirit of mine did with the least affection of a welcome give entertainment to the might of it

Let God for ever keep it from my head and make me as the poorest vassal is that doth with awe and terror kneel to it!

King Henry IV

Oh my son, God put it in thy mind to take it hence,

That thou mightst win the more thy father's love, pleading so wisely in excuse of it!

Come hither, Harry, sit thou by my bed

Hear, I think, the very latest counsel that ever I shall breathe.

God knows, my son, by what by-paths and indirect crooked ways I met this crown

I myself know well how troublesome it sat upon my head.

To thee it shall descend with bitter quiet, better opinion, better confirmation

For all the soil of the achievement goes with me into the earth. It seemed in me but as an honour snatched with boisterous hand, and I had many living to upbraid my gain of it by their assistances

Which daily grew to quarrel and to bloodshed, wounding supposed peace, all these bold fears thou see'st with peril I have answered

For all my reign hath been but as a scene acting that argument, and now my death changes the mode

What in me was purchased falls upon thee in a more fairer sort

So thou the garland wear'st successively.

Yet, though thou stand'st more sure than I could do, thou art not firm enough, since griefs are green

All my friends, which thou must make thy friends, have but their stings and teeth newly taken out

By whose fell working I was first advanced and by whose power I well might lodge a fear to be again displaced: which to avoid, I cut them off

Had a purpose now to lead out many to the Holy Land, lest rest and lying still might make them look too near unto my state

Therefore, my Harry, be it thy course to busy giddy minds with foreign quarrels; that action, hence borne out, may waste the memory of the former days.

More would I, but my lungs are wasted so that strength of speech is utterly denied me.

How I came by the crown, oh God forgive

Grant it may with thee in true peace live!

Prince Henry

My gracious liege, you won it, wore it, kept it, gave it me

Then plain and right must my possession be, which I with more than with a common pain against all the world will rightfully maintain.

(Lord John of Lancaster enters)

King Henry IV

Look, look, here comes my John of Lancaster.

Lancaster

Health, peace, and happiness to my royal father!

King Henry IV

Thou bring'st me happiness and peace, son John

Health, alack, with youthful wings is flown from this bare withered trunk, upon thy sight my worldly business makes a period.

Where is my Lord of Warwick?

Prince Henry

My Lord of Warwick!

(Warkwick, and others enter)

King Henry IV

Doth any name particular belong unto the lodging where I first did swoon?

Warkwick

It is called Jerusalem, my noble lord.

King Henry IV

Laud be to God! even there my life must end.

It hath been prophesied to me many years, I should not die but in Jerusalem

Which vainly I supposed the Holy Land, but bear me to that chamber

There I'll lie

In that Jerusalem shall Harry die.

(Exit)

Act 5 Scene 1

Gloucestershire. Shallow's house.

(Shallow, Falstaff, Bardolph, and Page enter)

Shallow

By cock and pie, sir, you shall not away to-night.

What, Davy, I say!

Falstaff

You must excuse me, Master Robert Shallow.

Shallow

I will not excuse you; you shall not be excused

Excuses shall not be admitted; there is no excuse shall serve

You shall not be excused.

Why, Davy!

(Davy enters)

Davy

Here, sir.

Shallow

Davy, Davy, Davy, Davy, let me see Davy

Let me see Davy

Let me see, yea, marry, William cook, bid him come hither.

Sir John, you shall not be excused.

Davy

Marry, sir, thus

Those precepts cannot be served, and again sir, shall we sow the headland with wheat?

Shallow

With red wheat, Davy.

But for William cook, are there no young pigeons?

Davy

Yes, sir. Here is now the smith's note for shoeing and plough-irons.

Shallow

Let it be cast and paid. Sir John, you shall not be excused.

Davy

Now, sir, a new link to the bucket must need be had, and sir, do you mean to stop any of William's wages, about the sack he lost the other day at Hinckley fair?

Shallow

A' shall answer it.

Some pigeons, Davy, a couple of short-legged hens, a joint of mutton, and any pretty little tiny kickshaws, tell William cook.

Davy

Doth the man of war stay all night, sir?

Shallow

Yea, Davy.

I will use him well, a friend in the court is better than a penny in purse.

Use his men well, Davy

For they are arrant knaves, and will backbite

Davy

No worse than they are backbitten, sir

For they have marvellous foul linen.

Shallow

Well conceited Davy, about thy business Davy.

Davy

I beseech you, sir, to countenance William Visor of Woncot against Clement Perkes of the hill.

Shallow

There is many complaints Davy, against that Visor, that Visor is an arrogant knave, on my knowledge.

Davy

I grant your worship that he is a knave, sir

Yet, God forbid, sir, but a knave should have some countenance at his friend's request.

An honest man sir, is able to speak for himself, when a knave is not.

I have served your worship truly sir, this eight years

If I cannot once or twice in a quarter bear out a knave against an honest man, I have but a very little credit with your worship.

The knave is mine honest friend, sir

Therefore, I beseech your worship, let him be countenanced.

Shallow

Go to

I say he shall have no wrong.

Look about, Davy.

(Davy exits)

Where are you, Sir John?

Come, come, come, off with your boots.

Give me your hand, Master Bardolph.

Bardolph

I am glad to see your worship.

Shallow

I thank thee with all my heart, kind Master Bardolph and welcome, my tall fellow.

(To the Page)

Come, Sir John.

Falstaff

I'll follow you, good Master Robert Shallow.

(Shallow exits)

Bardolph, look to our horses.

(Bardolph and Page exit)

If I were sawed into quantities, I should make four dozen of such bearded hermits' staves as Master Shallow.

It is a wonderful thing to see the semblable coherence of his men's spirits and his, they by observing of him, do bear themselves like foolish justices

He, by conversing with them is turned into a justice-like serving-man, their spirits are so married in conjunction with the participation of society that they flock together in consent, like so many wild-geese.

If I had a suit to Master Shallow, I would humour his men with the imputation of being near their master: if to his men, I would curry with Master Shallow that no man could better command his servants.

It is certain that either wise bearing or ignorant carriage is caught, as men take diseases, one of another, therefore let men take heed of their company.

I will devise matter enough out of this Shallow to keep Prince Harry in continual laughter the wearing out of six fashions, which is four terms, or two actions, and a' shall laugh without intervallums.

Oh, it is much that a lie with a slight oath and a jest with a sad brow will do with a fellow that never had the ache in his shoulders!

Oh, you shall see him laugh till his face be like a wet cloak ill laid up!

Shallow

(From Within) Sir John!

Falstaff

I come, Master Shallow; I come, Master Shallow.

(Exits)

Act 5 Scene 2

Westminster. The palace.

(Warkwick and the Lord Chief-Justice enter, meeting)

Warkwick

How now, my lord chief-justice! whither away?

Lord Chief-Justice

How doth the king?

Warkwick

Exceeding well; his cares are now all ended.

Lord Chief-Justice

I hope, not dead.

Warkwick

He's walk'd the way of nature

To our purposes he lives no more.

Lord Chief-Justice

I would his majesty had called me with him, the service that I truly did his life hath left me open to all injuries.

Warkwick

Indeed I think the young king loves you not.

Lord Chief-Justice

I know he doth not, and do arm myself to welcome the condition of the time, which cannot look more hideously upon me than I have drawn it in my fantasy.

(Lancaster, Clarence, Gloucester, Westmoreland, and others enter)

Warkwick

Here come the heavy issue of dead Harry, oh that the living Harry had the temper of him, the worst of these three gentlemen!

How many nobles then should hold their places that must strike sail to spirits of vile sort!

Lord Chief-Justice

Oh God, I fear all will be overturned!

Lancaster

Good morrow, cousin Warwick, good morrow.

Gloucester Clarence

Good morrow, cousin.

Lancaster

We meet like men that had forgot to speak.

Warkwick

We do remember

Our argument is all too heavy to admit much talk.

Lancaster

Well, peace be with him that hath made us heavy.

Lord Chief-Justice

Peace be with us, lest we be heavier!

Gloucester

Oh good my lord, you have lost a friend indeed

I dare swear you borrow not that face of seeming sorrow, it is sure your own.

Lancaster

Though no man be assured what grace to find you stand in coldest expectation

I am the sorrier

Would it were otherwise.

Clarence

Well, you must now speak Sir John Falstaff fair

Which swims against your stream of quality.

Lord Chief-Justice

Sweet princes, what I did, I did in honour, led by the impartial conduct of my soul, and never shall you see that I will beg a ragged and forestalled remission.

If truth and upright innocency fail me, I'll to the king my master that is dead, and tell him who hath sent me after him.

Warkwick

Here comes the prince.

(King Henry V enters, attended)

Lord Chief-Justice

Good morrow

God save your majesty!

King Henry V

This new and gorgeous garment, majesty, sits not so easy on me as you think.

Brothers, you mix your sadness with some fear, this is the English, not the Turkish court

Not Amurath an Amurath succeeds, but Harry Harry.

Yet be sad, good brothers, for by my faith, it very well becomes you, sorrow so royally in you appears that I will deeply put the fashion on and wear it in my heart, why then be sad

Entertain no more of it, good brothers, than a joint burden laid upon us all.

For me, by heaven, I bid you be assured I'll be your father and your brother too

Let me but bear your love, I 'll bear your cares, yet weep that Harry's dead

So will I

Harry lives, that shall convert those tears by number into hours of happiness.

Princes

We hope no other from your majesty.

King Henry V

You all look strangely on me, and you most

You are, I think, assured I love you not.

Lord Chief-Justice

I am assured, if I be measured rightly, your majesty hath no just cause to hate me.

King Henry V

No!

How might a prince of my great hopes forget so great indignities you laid upon me?

What! rate, rebuke, and roughly send to prison the immediate heir of England!

Was this easy?

May this be washed in Lethe, and forgotten?

Lord Chief-Justice

I then did use the person of your father

The image of his power lay then in me, and in the administration of his law, whiles I was busy for the commonwealth your highness pleased to forget my place

The majesty and power of law and justice, the image of the king whom I presented and struck me in my very seat of judgment

Whereon, as an offender to your father, I gave bold way to my authority and did commit you.

If the deed were ill, be you contented wearing now the garland, to have a son set your decrees and nought to pluck down justice from your awful bench, to trip the course of law and blunt the sword that guards the peace and safety of your person

Nay, more, to spurn at your most royal image and mock your workings in a second body

Question your royal thoughts, make the case yours

Be now the father and propose a son, hear your own dignity so much profaned, see your most dreadful laws so loosely slighted, behold yourself so by a son disdained

Then imagine me taking your part and in your power soften silencing your son, after this cold considerance, sentence me

As you are a king, speak in your state what I have done that misbecame my place, my person, or my liege's sovereignty.

King Henry V

You are right, justice, and you weigh this well

Therefore still bear the balance and the sword, and I do wish your honours may increase, till you do live to see a son of mine offend you and obey you, as I did.

So shall I live to speak my father's words, happy am I, that have a man so bold that dares do justice on my proper son

Not less happy, having such a son, that would deliver up his greatness so into the hands of justice.

You did commit me, for which I do commit into your hand the unstained sword that you have used to bear

With this remembrance, that you use the same with the like bold, just and impartial spirit as you have done against me.

There is my hand.

You shall be as a father to my youth, my voice shall sound as you do prompt mine ear and I will stoop and humble my intents to your well-practised wise directions.

And, princes all, believe me, I beseech you

My father is gone wild into his grave for in his tomb lie my affections

With his spirit sadly I survive, to mock the expectation of the world, to frustrate prophecies and to raze out rotten opinion who hath writ me down after my seeming.

The tide of blood in me hath proudly flowed in vanity till now, now doth it turn and web back to the sea where it shall mingle with the state of floods and flow henceforth in formal majesty.

Now call we our high court of parliament, and let us choose such limbs of noble counsel that the great body of our state may go in equal rank with the best governed nation

That war, or peace, or both at once, may be as things acquainted and familiar to us

In which you, father, shall have foremost hand.

Our coronation done, we will accite, as I before remembered all our state, and God consigning to my good intents, no prince nor peer shall have just cause to say God shorten Harry's happy life one day!

(Exit)

Act 5 Scene 3

Gloucestershire. Shallow's orchard.

(Falstaff, Shallow, Silence, Davy, Bardolph, and the Page enter)

Shallow

Nay, you shall see my orchard, where, in an arbour, we will eat a last year's pippin of my own graffing with a dish of caraways, and so forth

Come cousin Silence, and then to bed.

Falstaff

Before God, you have here a goodly dwelling and a rich.

Shallow

Barren, barren, barren

Beggars all, beggars all

Sir John, marry good air.

Spread Davy

Spread, Davy

Well said, Davy.

Falstaff

This Davy serves you for good uses

He is your serving-man and your husband.

Shallow

A good varlet, a good varlet, a very good varlet

Sir John, by the mass, I have drunk too much sack at supper, a good varlet.

Now sit down, now sit down, come cousin.

Silence

Ah, sirrah! quoth-a, we shall do nothing but eat, and make good cheer,

(Singing)

And praise God for the merry year

When flesh is cheap and females dear

And lusty lads roam here and there

So merrily, and ever among so merrily

Falstaff

There's a merry heart!

Good Master Silence, I'll give you a health for that anon.

Shallow

Give Master Bardolph some wine, Davy.

Davy

Sweet sir, sit

I'll be with you anon. most sweet sir, sit

Master page, good master page, sit.

Proface! What you want in meat, we'll have in drink, but you must bare… the heart's all.

(Exits)

Shallow

Be merry, Master Bardolph

My little soldier, there, be merry.

Silence

Be merry, be merry, my wife has all

(Singing)

For women are shrews, both short and tall

It is merry in hall when beards wag all

And welcome merry Shrove-tide.

Be merry, be merry.

Falstaff

I did not think Master Silence had been a man of this mettle.

Silence

Who, I? I have been merry twice and once ere now.

(Davy re-enters)

Davy

(To Bardolph)

There's a dish of leather-coats for you.

Shallow

Davy!

Davy

Your worship! I'll be with you straight.

(To Bardolph)

A cup of wine, sir?

Silence

A cup of wine that's brisk and fine,

(Singing)

And drink unto the leman mine

And a merry heart lives long-a.

Falstaff

Well said, Master Silence.

Silence

And we shall be merry, now comes in the sweet of the night.

Falstaff

Health and long life to you, Master Silence.

Silence

Fill the cup, and let it come

(Singing)

I'll pledge you a mile to the bottom.

Shallow

Honest Bardolph, welcomem if thou wantest any thing and wilt not call, beshrew thy heart.

Welcome, my little tiny thief.

(To the Page)

And welcome indeed too.

I'll drink to Master Bardolph, and to all the cavaleros about London.

Davy

I love to see London once before I die.

Bardolph

And I might see you there, Davy...

Shallow

By the mass, you'll crack a quart together, ha!

Will you not, Master Bardolph?

Bardolph

Yea, sir, in a pottle-pot.

Shallow

By God's liggens, I thank thee: the knave will stick by thee, I can assure thee that.

He will not out

He is true bred.

Bardolph

And I'll stick by him, sir.

Shallow

Why, there spoke a king.

Lack nothing, be merry.

(Knocking within)

Look who's at door there, who! who knocks?

(Davy exits)

Falstaff

Why, now you have done me right.

(To Silence, seeing him take off a bumper)

Silence

(Singing)

Do me right, and dub me knight, Samingo.

Is it not so?

Falstaff

It is so.

Silence

Is it so? Why then, say an old man can do somewhat.

(Davy re-enters)

Davy

And if it please your worship, there's one Pistol come from the court with news.

Falstaff

From the court! let him come in.

(Pistol enters)

How now, Pistol!

Pistol

Sir John, God save you!

Falstaff

What wind blew you hither, Pistol?

Pistol

Not the ill wind which blows no man to good.

Sweet knight, thou art now one of the greatest men in this realm.

Silence

By your lady, I think you be, but goodman Puff of Barson.

Pistol

Puff!

Puff in thy teeth, most recreant coward base!

Sir John, I am thy Pistol and thy friend and helter-skelter have I rode to thee, and tidings do I bring and lucky joys, and golden times and happy news of price.

Falstaff

I pray thee now, deliver them like a man of this world.

Pistol

A foutre for the world and worldlings base!

I speak of Africa and golden joys.

Falstaff

Oh base Assyrian knight, what is thy news?

Let King Cophetua know the truth thereof.

Silence

And Robin Hood, Scarlet, and John.

(Singing)

Pistol

Shall dunghill curs confront the Helicons?

And shall good news be baffled?

Then, Pistol, lay thy head in Furies' lap.

Silence

Honest gentleman, I know not your breeding.

Pistol

Why then, lament therefore.

Shallow

Give me pardon sir, if sir you come with news from the court, I take it there's but two ways, either to utter them, or to conceal them.

I am sir, under the king, in some authority.

Pistol

Under which king, Besonian? speak, or die.

Shallow

Under King Harry.

Pistol

Harry the Fourth? or Fifth?

Shallow

Harry the Fourth.

Pistol

A foutre for thine office!

Sir John, thy tender lambkin now is king;

Harry a fifth's the man.

I speak the truth, when Pistol lies, do this

Fig me, like the bragging Spaniard.

Falstaff

What, is the old king dead?

Pistol

As nail in door, the things I speak are just.

Falstaff

Away, Bardolph! Saddle my horse.

Master Robert Shallow, choose what office thou wilt in the land, it is thine.

Pistol, I will double-charge thee with dignities.

Bardolph

Oh joyful day!

I would not take a knighthood for my fortune.

Pistol

What! I do bring good news.

Falstaff

Carry Master Silence to bed. Master Shallow, my

Lord Shallow...

Be what thou wilt

I am fortune's steward…

Get on thy boots: we'll ride all night.

Oh sweet Pistol! Away, Bardolph!

(Bardolph exits)

Come, Pistol, utter more to me; and withal devise something to do thyself good.

Boot, boot, Master Shallow

I know the young king is sick for me.

Let us take any man's horses

The laws of England are at my commandment.

Blessed are they that have been my friends

Woe to my lord chief-justice!

Pistol

Let vultures vile seize on his lungs also!

Where is the life that late I led? say they, why here it is

Welcome these pleasant days!

(Exit)

Act 5 Scene 4

London. A street.

(Beadles enters, dragging in Hostess Quickly and Doll Tearsheet)

Mistress Quickly

No, thou arrant knave

I would to God that I might die, that I might have thee hanged, thou hast drawn my shoulder out of joint.

First Beadle

The constables have delivered her over to me

She shall have whipping-cheer enough, I warrant her, there hath been a man or two lately killed about her.

Doll Tearsheet

Nut-hook, nut-hook, you lie.

Come on

I'll tell thee what, thou damned tripe-visaged rascal, and the child I now go with do miscarry, thou wert better thou hadst struck thy mother, thou paper-faced villain.

Mistress Quickly

Oh the Lord, that Sir John were come!

He would make this a bloody day to somebody.

I pray God the fruit of her womb miscarry!

First Beadle

If it do, you shall have a dozen of cushions again

You have but eleven now.

Come, I charge you both go with me

For the man is dead that you and Pistol beat amongst you.

Doll Tearsheet

I'll tell you what, you thin man in a censer, I will have you as soundly swinged for this...

You blue-bottle rogue, you filthy famished correctioner, if you be not swinged, I'll forswear half-kirtles.

First Beadle

Come, come, you she knight-errant, come.

Mistress Quickly

Oh God, that right should thus overcome might!

Well, of sufferance comes ease.

Doll Tearsheet

Come, you rogue, come; bring me to a justice.

Mistress Quickly

Ay, come, you starved blood-hound.

Doll Tearsheet

Goodman death, goodman bones!

Mistress Quickly

Thou atomy, thou!

Doll Tearsheet

Come, you thin thing; come you rascal.

First Beadle

Very well.

(Exit)

Act 5 Scene 5

A public place near Westminster Abbey.

(Grooms enter, strewing rushes)

First Groom

More rushes, more rushes.

Second Groom

The trumpets have sounded twice.

First Groom

It will be two o'clock ere they come from the coronation: dispatch, dispatch.

(Exit)

(Falstaff, Shallow, Pistol, Bardolph, and Page enter)

Falstaff

Stand here by me, Master Robert Shallow

I will make the king do you grace, I will leer upon him as a' comes by

Do but mark the countenance that he will give me.

Pistol

God bless thy lungs, good knight.

Falstaff

Come here, Pistol

Stand behind me

Oh, if I had had time to have made new liveries, I would have bestowed the thousand pound I borrowed of you.

But it is no matter

This poor show doth better, this doth infer the zeal I had to see him.

Shallow

It doth so.

Falstaff

It shows my earnestness of affection...

Shallow

It doth so.

Falstaff

My devotion...

Shallow

It doth, it doth, it doth.

Falstaff

As it were, to ride day and night; and not to deliberate, not to remember, not to have patience to shift me...

Shallow

It is best, certain.

Falstaff

But to stand stained with travel, and sweating with desire to see him; thinking of nothing else, putting all affairs else in oblivion, as if there were nothing else to be done but to see him.

Pistol

It is that's how it is, nothing else matters, it is all in every part.

Shallow

It is so, indeed.

Pistol

My knight, I will inflame thy noble liver, and make thee rage.

Thy Doll, and Helen of thy noble thoughts, is in base durance and contagious prison

Haled thither by most mechanical and dirty hand, rouse up revenge from your good den with fallen Alecto's snake, for Doll is in.

Pistol speaks nought but truth.

Falstaff

I will deliver her.

(Shouts within, and the trumpets sound)

Pistol

There roared the sea, and trumpet-clangor sounds.

(King Henry V and his train enters, the Lord Chief- Justice among them)

Falstaff

God save thy grace, King Hal! my royal Hal!

Pistol

The heavens thee guard and keep, most royal imp of fame!

Falstaff

God save thee, my sweet boy!

King Henry IV

My lord chief-justice, speak to that vain man.

Lord Chief-Justice

Have you your wits? know you what it is to speak?

Falstaff

My king! my Jupiter I speak to thee, my heart!

King Henry IV

I know thee not, old man, fall to thy prayers

How ill white hairs become a fool and jester!

I have long dreamed of such a kind of man, so surfeit-swell'd, so old and so profane

Being awaked, I do despise my dream.

Make less thy body hence, and more thy grace

Leave gormandizing

Know the grave doth gape for thee thrice wider than for other men.

Reply not to me with a fool-born jest, presume not that I am the thing I was

For God doth know, so shall the world perceive, that I have turn'd away my former self

So will I those that kept me company.

When thou dost hear I am as I have been, approach me, and thou shalt be as thou wast the tutor and the feeder of my riots

Till then, I banish thee, on pain of death, as I have done the rest of my misleaders, not to come near our person by ten mile.

For competence of life I will allow you, that lack of means enforce you not to evil, and as we hear you do reform yourselves we will, according to your strengths and qualities, give you advancement.

Be it your charge, my lord, to see performed the tenor of our word.

Set on.

(King Henry V & company exit)

Falstaff

Master Shallow, I owe you a thousand pound.

Shallow

Yea, marry, Sir John

I beseech you to let me have home with me.

Falstaff

That can hardly be, Master Shallow.

Do not you grieve at this

I shall be sent for in private to him, look you, he must seem thus to the world, fear not your advancements

I will be the man yet that shall make you great.

Shallow

I cannot well perceive how, unless you should give me your doublet and stuff me out with straw.

I beseech you, good Sir John, let me have five hundred of my thousand.

Falstaff

Sir, I will be as good as my word, this that you heard was but a colour.

Shallow

A colour that I fear you will die in, Sir John.

Falstaff

Fear no colours, go with me to dinner, come Lieutenant Pistol Come Bardolph, I shall be sent for soon at night.

(Prince John of Lancaster, the Lord Chief-Justice, and Officers with them enter)

Lord Chief-Justice

Go, carry Sir John Falstaff to the Fleet, take all his company along with him.

Falstaff

My lord, my lord...

Lord Chief-Justice

I cannot now speak, I will hear you soon.

Take them away.

Pistol

If fortune torments me, hope does contents me

(All but Prince John and the Lord Chief-Justice exit)

Lancaster

I like this fair proceeding of the king's, he hath intent his wonted followers shall all be very well provided for

All are banished till their conversations appear more wise and modest to the world.

Lord Chief-Justice

And so they are.

Lancaster

The king hath called his parliament, my lord.

Lord Chief-Justice

He hath.

Lancaster

I will lay odds that, ere this year expire, we bear our civil swords and native fire as far as France: I beard a bird so sing, whose music, to my thinking, pleased the king.

Come, will you hence?

(Exit)

Finally

(Spoken by a Dancer)

First my fear

Then my courtesy

Last my speech.

My fear is your displeasure

My courtesy is my duty

My speech is to beg your pardons.

If you look for a good speech now, you undo me, for what I have to say is of mine own making

What indeed I should say will, I doubt, prove mine own marring.

But to the purpose, and so to the venture.

Be it known to you, as it is very well, I was lately here in the end of a displeasing play, to pray your patience for it and to promise you a better.

I meant indeed to pay you with this

If like an ill venture it come unluckily home, I break, and

you, my gentle creditors, lose.

Here I promised you I would be and here I commit my body to your mercies, bate me some and I will pay you some and, as most debtors do, promise you infinitely.

If my tongue cannot entreat you to acquit me, will you command me to use my legs?

And yet that were but light payment, to dance out of your debt.

But a good conscience will make any possible satisfaction, and so would I.

All the gentlewomen here have forgiven me, if the gentlemen will not, then the gentlemen do not agree with the gentlewomen, which was never seen before in such an assembly.

One word more, I beseech you.

If you be not too much cloyed with fat meat, our humble author will continue the story, with Sir John in it, and make you merry with fair Katharine of France, where for anything I know, Falstaff shall die of a sweat, unless already a' be killed with your hard opinions

For Oldcastle died a martyr, and this is not the man

My tongue is weary

When my legs are too, I will bid you good night, and so kneel down before you

Indeed, to pray for the queen.

The End

Description of Titles

The Comedy of Errors
Caught in a land of embittered woman and war, caught in months of strife, where a merchant's visit offers little natural relief. The fleeting moment of approving gold, inspire further bitterness, upon an approach to the marketplace, and then the women that occupy within them.

19 Characters

The Taming of the Shrew
Arrangements are made to spencer would be suiters to melt the splendors of a strong willed women. The winning is found pledged, influencing maids to seek their turns, and meanwhile terms required, an authentic spirit that they will/would wed soon. **34 Characters**

Love's Labor's Lost
The house of a scholarly pursuit, returns into an expressive, either poetic or drunken as highlighting the gold-slur filled house of charms and dance like rhymes

19 Characters

A Midsummer Night's Dream
Journey into a land of fairies, where creatures are found to have the same issues as nobilities. Exemplifying, perhaps, there's no place like home. Meet fairies as they frolic and play the noble hearts and sway, posed in the recesses of night, and mystic lands of a faraway kingdom.

22 Characters

The Merchant of Venice

An angry Shylock brings to trial a merchant, over a lover's quarrel disrupted, demanding pounds of flesh. With no desires for even three times the amount, the Shylock demands his vengeance at heart.

22 Characters

The Merry Wives of Windsor
Mistresses and lords try and relate towards one another, as various important community figures come to have their word/seek the hostesses. Pleasantries are exchanged as a range of charms are expressed, until conversation resembled so to folly.

23 Characters

Much Ado About Nothing
Soldiery level consideration occupy the gossip, as several hostilities are summoned up, onto heart related matter. Also in conflict. The latter portion of the story lightens up to a women's home and pleasantries. Thereafter, a general search and care in actions, creating response phrasing poetic to the responses of leadership parading, until an end full of sensitivity asking gently questions, onto kisses

23 Characters

As You Like It
Troubled lower nobles venture about daily business, with some mild graces towards the ladies found. In need of relief or play, the Duke and family members take to the woods, where jests of drinking turn into troubled amusements, or warmth of a women's heart.   **26 Characters**

Troilus and Cressida

The infamous Greek battle for Troy. A large army arrives to take back the lost love of a humiliated foe. Both sides mobilize heroes onto the field, as soldiers and generals move to the side, and let strategies and fate take their course.

21+ Characters

All's Well That Ends Well

A tale of delightful, womanly gossip of a prestigious sort, until the French King has his word on the excellence of others. The story initially revolves around a strong willed countess, whose courteous pose and insight, reflect a nobility reflective of the house and court (council). Dialogue therein revolving around the councils rather, to exemplify (court counselling women).

25 Characters

Measure for Measure

Statesmen discourse leading with time to a personal reflection. Strolling Dukes and strong willed women occupy the background, where high-function status and family discourse intertwine within formalities (of administrative foresight, expression) observed.

24 Characters

Richard III

An in palace drama with King Richard the 3rd, Queen Elizabeth, and Queen Margret. Onto a haunting reunion, as the state processes royal executions.

61+ Characters

The Life and Death of King John

King John and Queen Elinor entertain the royal court, where a bastard has come to make his day. Strategic deployments of influence are exemplified, as the bastard plots about until alerts, alarm corruption has delivered trouble makers known.

24 Characters

Romeo and Juliet

Lovers emerge within a city gripped with two feuding houses apposed. As turmoil are caught in bitter heat, the lover's. Bliss and undying pledge becomes them, onto the eternal soul (of love and romance).

33 Characters

Othello

A hopeful Othello calls upon the favor of allies based on proposed merits, which called upon allies and foes to him. In a mixed response, allies and foes campaign both against Othello, becoming a bitter, personal tangle over a mislead love adventure representing the future of either fates

25 Characters

Macbeth

A desperate Macbeth ventures towards witches to tell fortune, returning to a castle haunted by ghost/old-spirits. Macbeth's worries become frightful nightmares, along the despair of the household around him.

39 Characters

Mark Antony and Cleopatra

The relations or affections of Mark Anthony and Cleopatra, onto the strategic interactions between Mark Anthony and Octavius. The discourse moves to the Octavius house, revealing Octavia, and later then, Pompey in the background. Overall the focus retains upon Mark Anthony, Cleopatra, and Octavius.

56+ Characters

Coriolanus

Citizens riot during a famine, while the state administrative intervenes and otherwise discourses the seriousness of the matter and war. Lady's calm the general ambience, until the sword is mobilized to defend the gates, , while the plight of people is nevertheless heard convincing Roman elites the problem is being found/fought within.

60 Characters

Pericles Prince of Tyre

A thoughtful/reflective Pericles interposes his good will and well-meaning nature, which leads him to visit fishermen friends, and onto state function. Pericles is then confronted, required to (take a plunge) to marry, embedding him deeper into ocean stock of sea life among sailors experience and merchant owners, investing his interest as babe, securing his destiny as then, future king   **44 Characters**

Cymbeline

Cymbeline, friend or loyalist to the first Caesars, is summoned into battle. Meanwhile there are personal matters to attend to within the noble house.

41 Characters

The Winter's Tale

A gossipy tale of high office, administrative daily insight onto the tender meaning of things and people an how they unite unwittingly at the discourse of their respected hierarchies of partnership. Profoundness therein inspiring the recounts of clown and child, as examples perhaps of what state administration and or nobility's company keeps.

34+ Characters

The Tempest
After an earth shattering storm, a fairy dwelling world is found. There magic and graces are there in song, glory and praises.

21 Characters

The Two Gentlemen of Verona
Loving beginnings, yet far too. General virtues going upwards in hierarchies, with overall chivalrous wits.

Twelfth Night
An evening in the company of sound gatherings, seemingly a docile manner recount version of noble delights. In similarities of the pose, composing an environment of insight and oversight.

Henry the 8th
Across chamber and palace, Dukes and lords, until Queen Katharine's and King Henry VIII's present their graces, conversing the Cardinal then. The signs then, an Elizabeth is born.

Richard II
King Richard the 2nd readies the armed forces at the sound of alarm, while later Henry IV is near for discussion. King Richard the 2nd and his groom.

Henry V
King Henry the 5th, as found across his palace, until a readiness for war. King Henry the 5th and the French King, with armies both have at it.

Henry VI, Part 1
Funeral of King Henry the 5th, Henry VI makes his approach to France. Henry VI fashions as thy lord protector.

Henry VI, Part 2
King Henry the 6th, where the Cardinal is seen mocking protectors with praise, as all the rage. Queen Margaret at King Henry VI, until the end.

Henry VI, Part 3
King Henry VI is busy fighting a succession of battles, France and England as having at it, yet again.

King Henry the 5th
King Henry 5 fight his way toward France, they reach the peaceful and loving responses of a French King.

Henry IV, Part 1
King Henry the 4th, from Palace to Pub, onto the battle fields again. Until there is no rebellion.

Henry IV, Part 2
Henry IV, from Palace, Priest and then tavern, he nevertheless finds some peace, after reflection. King Henry IV, and then King Henry V as fashionable by the end.

Titus Andronicus
A story of Romans and Goths, where roman sways give way. And then to see about Goths and proving worthiness.

28 Characters

Julius Caesar

Near the Final days of the 1st Caesar, and the continuation everlasting as through Octavius.

Hamlet
Hamlet, and his father the King, the father yet a Ghost. Hamlet, not so eager to join.

King Lear
King Lear, from palace to castle, to fighting the French in the field. After battle King Lear is in bed, the Doctor discourses, what lays then now, will have an impact upon the end.

Timon of Athens
A story set in Greece, a place of poets and cultured, good graces. From Arts and daily expressive, to political and charmed.